TEENAGERS DIGITAL SAFETY IN THE ERA OF AI & DEEPFAKES

A HANDBOOK TO SAFEGUARD EVERY TEENAGER IN THE DIGITAL AGE

ASHISH GUPTA

To my beloved family and friends, whose unwavering support and encouragement have been the cornerstone of my journey. Your belief in me has been a constant source of strength and inspiration.

To all the students striving for knowledge and personal growth, may this book serve as a guide and companion on your path to success.

And to the educators and mentors who dedicate their lives to shaping the minds of future generations, thank you for your invaluable contributions and tireless efforts. This book is a tribute to your enduring impact and dedication.

Contents

Contents

Contents

Contents

Preface

In an age where technology evolves at a dizzying pace, our lives are increasingly intertwined with digital innovations that offer both incredible opportunities and significant challenges. Among the most vulnerable in this rapidly changing digital landscape are teenagers, who are growing up with unprecedented access to information, social networks, and digital platforms. While these technologies provide powerful tools for learning, social interaction, and entertainment, they also present unique risks that can have profound implications on the lives of young people.

This book, **"Teenagers' Digital Safety in the Era of AI & Deepfakes,"** is dedicated to empowering teens, parents, and educators to navigate the complexities of the digital world safely and responsibly. As Artificial Intelligence (AI) and deepfake technology become more sophisticated, understanding how to protect oneself from new and emerging threats is more critical than ever.

AI has brought remarkable advancements in various fields, including healthcare, education, and entertainment. However, it has also introduced new forms of cyber threats and privacy concerns. Deepfakes, a technology that uses AI to create hyper-realistic but fake videos and images, have added a new layer of complexity to digital safety. These fabricated visuals can be used to spread misinformation, manipulate public opinion, and even commit fraud, posing serious risks to the credibility of information and the privacy of individuals.

The rise of deepfakes underscores the importance of digital literacy and critical thinking. Teens must learn to discern between authentic and manipulated content, understand the potential misuse of their digital footprint, and protect their online identity. This book aims to provide practical guidance, tools, and resources to help them do just that.

Inside these pages, you will find comprehensive information on various aspects of digital safety. We begin by exploring the digital habits of teenagers and the platforms they frequently use, shedding light on the potential risks associated with each. We delve into the mechanics of AI and deepfake technology, offering insights into how these innovations work and the threats they pose. The book also covers essential topics such as data privacy, cyberbullying, online scams, and the ethical use of technology.

Moreover, this book emphasizes the critical role of parents and educators in guiding teenagers through the digital realm. By fostering open communication, setting appropriate boundaries, and encouraging responsible online behavior, adults can help teens develop a healthy relationship with technology.

As we venture deeper into the digital age, we must equip our youth with the knowledge and skills to navigate this new terrain safely. "Teenagers' Digital Safety in the Era of AI & Deepfakes" is not just a guidebook; it is a call to action for all of us to become more vigilant, informed, and proactive in ensuring a safer digital world for the next generation.

I hope this book serves as a valuable resource for teenagers, parents, and educators alike, empowering them to face the digital challenges of today and tomorrow with confidence and resilience.

Ashish Gupta (15th July 2024)

Disclaimer

The content of this book is intended to provide general information and guidance on personal development, digital literacy, and the impact of emerging technologies. While every effort has been made to ensure the accuracy and completeness of the information provided, the author and publisher make no representations or warranties of any kind, express or implied, about the completeness, accuracy, reliability, suitability, or availability with respect to the book or the information, products, services, or related graphics contained in the book for any purpose. Any reliance you place on such information is therefore strictly at your own risk.

The views and opinions expressed in this book are those of the author and do not necessarily reflect the official policy or position of any other agency, organization, employer, or company. Examples and case studies within this book are fictitious or have been modified to protect privacy, and any resemblance to real persons, living or dead, or real events is purely coincidental.

The author and publisher are not responsible for any errors or omissions or for the results obtained from the use of this information. All information in this book is provided "as is," with no guarantee of completeness, accuracy, timeliness, or of the results obtained from the use of this information, and without warranty of any kind, express or implied, including, but not limited to, warranties of performance, merchantability, and fitness for a particular purpose.

In no event will the author or publisher be liable to any person or entity for any direct, indirect, incidental, special, exemplary, or consequential damages of any kind, including, but not limited to, lost profits, loss of data, or any other commercial damages or losses, arising out of or in connection with the use of this book or the information contained herein.

Readers are encouraged to seek professional advice where appropriate and should not rely solely on the information provided in this book for making any decisions. The author and publisher disclaim any liability, loss, or risk, personal or otherwise, that is incurred as a consequence, directly or indirectly, of the use and application of any of the contents of this book.

Overview

The digital landscape has become an integral part of our daily lives, fundamentally transforming how we communicate, learn, and entertain ourselves. For teenagers, the internet is not just a tool but a significant extension of their social and personal lives. However, alongside the immense benefits of digital connectivity come unprecedented risks, particularly with the advent of advanced technologies such as Artificial Intelligence (AI) and deepfakes.

AI has revolutionized numerous aspects of modern life, offering remarkable benefits in areas like healthcare, education, and entertainment. Yet, it has also introduced new challenges in maintaining digital safety. Deepfakes, which are AI-generated images and videos that can convincingly mimic real people, have added a new layer of complexity to the threats faced by digital users. These highly realistic forgeries can be used maliciously to spread misinformation, create fake news, and perpetrate fraud, posing significant risks to the integrity of information and the privacy of individuals.

As teenagers navigate this digital era, they are uniquely vulnerable to these evolving threats. Growing up in an environment where digital and physical realities are deeply intertwined, they often lack the experience and critical thinking skills necessary to discern and mitigate these risks. This makes it imperative to provide them with the knowledge and tools to protect themselves online.

"Teenagers‘ Digital Safety in the Era of AI & Deepfakes" aims to address this critical need. This book is designed to be a comprehensive guide for teenagers, their parents, and educators, offering insights into the digital habits of young people and the potential dangers lurking in their online activities. We explore the workings of AI and deepfake technology, shedding light on how these innovations can be both beneficial and harmful.

The book is structured to provide practical advice and strategies for ensuring digital safety. We begin by examining the internet usage patterns among teenagers, identifying the most popular platforms and apps, and discussing the specific risks associated with each. Understanding the digital environment that teenagers engage with daily is the first step in fostering a safer online experience.

Next, we delve into the technical aspects of AI and deepfakes. By demystifying these technologies, we hope to equip readers with the knowledge to recognize and respond to potential threats. This section also includes tips on identifying fake content and protecting personal information from being misused.

Cyberbullying, data privacy, and the ethical use of technology are other critical areas covered in this book. We provide guidance on how to handle cyberbullying, protect one's digital footprint, and understand the importance of data privacy in an age where personal information is a valuable commodity.

The role of parents and educators is also emphasized throughout the book. By fostering open communication, setting clear boundaries, and encouraging responsible online behavior, adults can play a pivotal role in guiding teenagers through the complexities of the digital world.

Finally, we highlight the importance of digital literacy and critical thinking. In a world where misinformation can spread like wildfire, the ability to critically evaluate information and make informed decisions is more important than ever. This book provides strategies for developing these essential skills, empowering teenagers to navigate the digital landscape confidently and safely.

"Teenagers' Digital Safety in the Era of AI & Deepfakes" is not just a guidebook; it is a call to action. It underscores the collective responsibility we all share in protecting the next generation from digital harm. By arming teenagers with the knowledge and tools they need to stay safe online, we can help them reap the benefits of the digital age while minimizing the risks.

As we embark on this journey together, I hope this book serves as a valuable resource, sparking conversations, fostering understanding, and ultimately, ensuring that our teenagers can navigate the digital world with confidence and security.

Ashish Gupta

15th July 2024

About The Author

Ashish Gupta is a distinguished educator and visionary, with a deep commitment to the growth and cultural renaissance of Bharat. With over a decade of experience in the education sector, Ashish has been at the forefront of innovation and leadership, shaping the future leaders of India. His journey, which began in 2011, has been marked by a relentless pursuit of excellence and a passion for understanding and influencing the evolving landscape of the country.

In his role as Director of Admissions and Outreach at RV University, Bengaluru, Ashish has been instrumental in attracting and nurturing talented individuals. His expertise in student counseling and innovative educational approaches have made him a beloved mentor among students and a respected professional among his peers. His ability to connect with young minds has significantly contributed to the university's reputation for excellence.

Ashish's work extends beyond the classroom. He is actively involved in training individuals, helping them realize their potential and navigate the rapidly changing socio-economic environment of India. His contributions to personal development, motivation, and career guidance are well-documented in his numerous published works. Ashish envisions an India that is a global leader, rooted in its rich cultural heritage while advancing in development and innovation.

In "Teenagers Digital Safety in the Era of AI & Deepfakes," Ashish brings his expertise and passion to a critical and timely subject. As AI and deepfake technologies evolve, the digital safety of teenagers has become a paramount concern. Ashish's deep understanding of both the educational and technological landscapes allows him to provide valuable insights and practical guidance to help teenagers navigate this complex digital era safely.

Ashish Gupta's dedication to education, personal development, and his broader vision for India's future make him a compelling and authoritative voice on the subject of digital safety. His commitment to fostering a safe and empowering digital environment for teenagers is a testament to his belief in their potential to shape a brighter future for Bharat and the world.

Introduction

CHAPTER I

On the Ground: Riya, Principal & Deepfake Video

Riya, a 16-year-old student from Bangalore, woke up to the familiar buzz of her smartphone alarm. As she stretched and reached for her phone, she quickly checked her notifications. Overnight, her Instagram feed had been flooded with new posts, stories, and messages. Among the notifications, she noticed a message from her best friend, Aarav, linking to a video titled, "Check out this crazy deepfake of our principal!" Intrigued, Riya tapped on the link.

The video showed their school principal, Mr. Rao, seemingly singing and dancing to a popular Bollywood song. Riya couldn't believe her eyes – Mr. Rao, known for his strict demeanor, would never do something so outlandish. She realized it had to be a deepfake, a term she had recently learned about in her computer science class. While the video was amusing, it also sparked a sense of unease. What if someone used this technology to create something harmful or misleading?

Later that day, during a free period, Riya and her friends gathered around the school courtyard, discussing the deepfake video. Aarav remarked, "It's funny now, but imagine if someone made a fake video about one of us and shared it everywhere. That could ruin someone's reputation."

Riya nodded thoughtfully, "Yes, it's scary how real these videos can look. We need to be careful about what we share and believe online."

Their conversation shifted to other ways AI was impacting their digital lives. Riya mentioned how she loved using AI filters on Instagram and Snapchat to enhance her photos and videos. "These filters are so cool, but I also think about how much data they must be collecting about our faces," she added.

Aarav agreed, "And not just filters. Even the ads we see on social media are influenced by AI. They know exactly what we like and show us those things."

Their friend, Neha, who was passionate about digital art, chimed in, "It's amazing how AI can help create art and animations, but we also need to know about the privacy risks. Our digital footprint is bigger than we think."

As the school day ended, Riya returned home and decided to spend some time online researching digital safety. She came across articles discussing the importance of strong passwords, two-factor authentication, and recognizing phishing attempts. She also learned about tools that could help detect deepfakes and safeguard personal information.

Feeling a mix of empowerment and responsibility, Riya decided to share her newfound knowledge with her friends. She created a group chat titled **"Digital Safety Squad"** and invited Aarav, Neha, and a few other close friends. In the chat, she posted tips and articles about staying safe online, understanding AI, and being mindful of the content they share and consume.

That evening, Riya's parents noticed her enthusiasm for digital safety and asked her about it. She explained what she had learned and how important it was for teenagers to be aware of the risks and benefits of AI and deepfakes. Her parents were impressed and encouraged her to keep exploring and educating others.

Over the next few weeks, Riya's Digital Safety Squad grew as more students joined in, eager to learn and share their experiences. They organized small workshops in their school, inviting guest speakers to talk about digital literacy, AI, and cybersecurity. The initiative not only educated students but also created a supportive community where they could discuss their digital concerns and find solutions together.

Riya's journey from a curious student to a digital safety advocate highlighted the critical need for awareness and education about AI and deepfakes. In an era where technology is deeply intertwined with their daily lives, Riya and her friends realized the importance of staying informed and vigilant. Their story serves as a reminder that while AI offers incredible opportunities, it also demands a proactive approach to ensuring a safe and secure digital environment for everyone.

Riya's story exemplifies the everyday challenges and opportunities Indian teens face in the digital age. As AI and deepfake technologies become more prevalent, understanding their impact and learning how to navigate the digital world safely is crucial. This book aims to equip teens with the knowledge and tools they need to protect themselves, make informed decisions, and harness the power of technology responsibly. Through examples, practical tips, and comprehensive insights, we will explore the multifaceted landscape of digital safety, empowering the next generation to thrive in the era of AI and deepfakes.

CHAPTER II

Understanding Digital Safety in the Age of AI

Digital safety, also known as online safety or internet safety, involves practices and precautions taken to protect personal information and ensure a safe and secure online experience. With the advent of AI, digital safety has become more complex and crucial.

The Impact of AI on Digital Safety - AI technology has revolutionized the digital landscape by enhancing user experiences and automating various tasks. However, it also introduces new risks and challenges. AI algorithms collect and analyze vast amounts of data, raising concerns about privacy and data security. Personal information can be misused if not properly protected. AI-driven personalization can create echo chambers and filter bubbles, influencing users' perceptions and behaviors. Targeted ads and recommendations may lead to exposure to inappropriate or harmful content.

AI can generate realistic but fake images, videos, and audio recordings, known as deepfakes. These can be used for malicious purposes, including misinformation and cyberbullying. AI-powered bots and malware can automate cyberattacks, making them more frequent and sophisticated. Phishing scams and other online threats are increasingly difficult to detect.

AI in Social Media and Online Platforms - AI is deeply

integrated into social media and other online platforms, impacting users' digital safety. AI algorithms help in moderating content, and detecting and removing harmful or inappropriate posts. Despite advancements, these systems are not foolproof and may fail to catch all harmful content.

AI analyzes user behavior to detect anomalies that might indicate security breaches or inappropriate activities. Continuous monitoring can lead to concerns about surveillance and privacy. AI-powered recommendation engines suggest content based on user preferences and behavior. These systems can unintentionally promote extremist content or misinformation.

Ensuring Digital Safety with AI - While AI presents new challenges, it also offers solutions to enhance digital safety. Advanced AI security tools can detect and respond to cyber threats in real time. AI can analyze patterns to identify potential vulnerabilities and prevent attacks.

AI algorithms designed to enhance privacy, such as differential privacy, help protect user data. Techniques like encryption and anonymization are essential for safeguarding personal information. Educating users about AI and digital safety practices is crucial. Awareness programs can help users recognize potential threats and adopt safe online behaviors.

Understanding digital safety in the age of AI requires a balanced approach that leverages AI's benefits while mitigating its risks. By staying informed and adopting proactive measures, teens can navigate the digital world safely and responsibly.

CHAPTER III

Why Focus on Indian Teens?

India has one of the largest youth populations in the world, with a significant percentage of its citizens being teenagers. This demographic is highly active online, making digital safety a critical concern. Indian teens are growing up in a digital-first environment, often more adept with technology than older generations, but they may lack awareness of the associated risks.

With increasing internet accessibility, even in rural areas, Indian teens are spending more time online. This widespread usage necessitates a focus on digital safety to protect young users. Many Indian teens access the internet primarily through smartphones, which poses unique security challenges, such as mobile malware and phishing attacks.

Indian family structures often include multi-generational households, where teens might help older family members navigate the digital world. This interdependency increases the need for teens to be knowledgeable about digital safety. While digital literacy is improving, many Indian schools still lack comprehensive programs on internet safety and AI, leaving teens unprepared for potential online threats. Indian teens are increasingly exposed to cyberbullying, which can have severe emotional and psychological impacts. With a rise in digital transactions, teens are vulnerable to online scams and fraud, requiring targeted education on safe online practices.

The Indian government is implementing policies to enhance digital security, but there is a need for educational initiatives that specifically address the challenges faced by teens. Understanding and complying with Indian cyber laws is crucial for teens to navigate the digital space safely and legally.

The mental health of Indian teens can be significantly affected by their online interactions. Ensuring digital safety is essential to protect their well-being. Focusing on digital safety helps foster critical thinking skills among teens, enabling them to make informed decisions and avoid potential online dangers.

Teaching digital safety to Indian teens equips them with the knowledge to handle online threats, fostering resilience and confidence in the digital world. By focusing on this demographic, we can cultivate a generation of responsible digital citizens who can contribute positively to the online community.

CHAPTER IV

Objectives of This Book

This book is focused on following 10 Key Objectives

1. Raise Awareness About Digital Safety

Educate Indian teens about the importance of digital safety and the potential risks associated with online activities & Highlight the impact of AI on digital safety and how it influences their online interactions.

2. Equip Teens with Practical Skills

Provide practical tips and strategies for protecting personal information and maintaining privacy online & Teach teens how to recognize and respond to cyber threats, such as phishing, malware, and online scams.

3. Promote Responsible Digital Behavior

Encourage responsible and ethical behavior in online interactions, including social media usage and content sharing & Emphasize the importance of creating a positive digital footprint and managing one's online reputation.

4. Enhance Digital Literacy

Improve teens' understanding of AI and its role in the digital world, including its benefits and potential risks & Foster critical thinking skills to help teens evaluate the credibility of online information and sources.

5. Support Mental Health and Well-being

Address the psychological impact of digital interactions, including cyberbullying and digital addiction & Provide guidance on balancing screen time with real-life activities to promote overall well-being.

6. Empower Parents and Educators

Offer resources and strategies for parents and educators to support teens in navigating the digital landscape safely & Encourage open communication between teens, parents, and educators about digital experiences and challenges.

7. Promote Legal and Ethical Awareness

Educate teens about their legal rights and responsibilities in the digital space under Indian cyber laws & Encourage adherence to ethical guidelines and responsible use of digital platforms.

8. Prepare Teens for Future Digital Challenges

Equip teens with the knowledge and skills to handle emerging digital challenges and advancements in AI technology & Foster adaptability and resilience to navigate the ever-evolving digital landscape.

9. Encourage Positive Digital Citizenship

Inspire teens to become proactive digital citizens who

contribute positively to the online community & Highlight the role of teens in shaping a safer and more inclusive digital environment.

10. Provide Resources for Continued Learning

Offer a comprehensive list of resources, including websites, tools, and further reading materials, to support ongoing learning about digital safety & Encourage teens to stay informed and updated on the latest digital safety practices and AI advancements.

The Digital Landscape in India

CHAPTER V

The Digital Journey of Ananya and Rohan

Ananya and Rohan, two high school students from Pune, represent the dynamic and rapidly evolving digital landscape of India. They live in a world where technology is woven into every aspect of their daily lives, from education to entertainment to social interactions.

A Typical Day - Ananya starts her day by checking her phone for updates on her favorite social media platforms, Instagram and WhatsApp. She scrolls through posts, likes her friends' pictures, and responds to messages. Meanwhile, Rohan prefers starting his day with a quick game of PUBG Mobile, engaging in a brief match before breakfast.

At school, Ananya and Rohan use their smartphones and tablets for educational purposes. Their teachers often incorporate digital tools into lessons, using apps and online resources to make learning more interactive and engaging. For example, during a history class, Ananya's teacher uses a VR app to take the class on a virtual tour of ancient Indian monuments. This immersive experience makes the lesson more vivid and memorable.

Online Learning and Digital Education - The COVID-19 pandemic accelerated the adoption of digital education in India. Ananya and Rohan experienced a significant shift as their school transitioned to online learning platforms.

They attended virtual classes via Zoom and Google Meet, submitted assignments on Google Classroom, and collaborated with classmates using Microsoft Team.

Rohan, who initially struggled with the transition, soon discovered the benefits of online learning. He appreciated the flexibility to learn at his own pace and access a wealth of resources beyond the traditional curriculum. Ananya, always a tech enthusiast, thrived in this environment, exploring additional courses on platforms like Coursera and Khan Academy to deepen her understanding of subjects like coding and artificial intelligence.

Social Media and Digital Connections - Social media plays a central role in Ananya and Rohan's social lives. They use platforms like Instagram, Snapchat, and TikTok to stay connected with friends, share moments, and express their creativity. Ananya, an aspiring artist, regularly posts her digital artwork on Instagram, gaining a following and even receiving feedback from established artists.

Rohan, on the other hand, enjoys creating funny TikTok videos. He collaborates with friends to produce content, participating in viral challenges and trends. These platforms offer them a space to showcase their talents, connect with like-minded individuals, and stay updated on global trends.

Gaming and Esports - Gaming is another significant aspect of their digital lives. Rohan is an avid gamer, spending his evenings playing popular games like PUBG Mobile, Free Fire, and Call of Duty Mobile. He dreams of becoming a professional esports player, inspired by the success stories of Indian gamers who have made a name for themselves on the international stage.

Ananya, although not as passionate about gaming, occasionally joins Rohan for a game of Among Us, enjoying the social aspect and teamwork involved. They both appreciate how gaming provides an avenue for relaxation and connection with friends.

Challenges and Opportunities - Despite the many advantages of digital technology, Ananya and Rohan are also aware of the challenges. They have encountered issues like cyberbullying, online scams, and the pressure to maintain a perfect online image. These experiences have taught them the importance of digital safety and the need to be cautious about sharing personal information online.

Their school has taken proactive steps to address these concerns, organizing workshops on digital literacy and online safety. Experts have been invited to talk about topics like recognizing fake news, protecting personal data, and dealing with cyberbullying. These initiatives have equipped Ananya, Rohan, and their peers with the knowledge and skills to navigate the digital world responsibly.

The Future of Digital India - As Ananya and Rohan look to the future, they are excited about the possibilities that technology holds. They dream of pursuing careers in fields like artificial intelligence, digital marketing, and cybersecurity. They are aware that the digital landscape is continuously evolving, and they are eager to be at the forefront of this change.

Their journey reflects the broader narrative of India's digital transformation. From urban centers to rural areas, technology is reshaping education, social interactions, entertainment, and career opportunities. For Ananya and Rohan, the digital world offers endless possibilities, and they are determined to make the most of it.

Ananya and Rohan's story highlights the diverse and dynamic nature of the digital landscape in India. It underscores the importance of digital literacy and safety while celebrating the opportunities that technology provides. As we delve deeper into this book, we will explore the various facets of digital life, offering insights and practical advice to help Indian teens navigate this exciting but complex world safely and effectively.

CHAPTER VI

Internet Usage Among Indian Teens

Indian teens are among the most active internet users globally, reflecting the rapid digital transformation in the country. This section explores the patterns, trends, and implications of internet usage among Indian teenagers.

Indian teens spend a significant portion of their day online, accessing the internet multiple times throughout the day. Social media, entertainment, and educational content are major draws. The majority of Indian teens access the internet via smartphones due to affordability and widespread availability. This mobile-first approach shapes their online behavior and experiences.

Platforms like Instagram, Facebook, Snapchat, and YouTube are highly popular among teens, who use these platforms to connect with friends, share content, and stay updated on trends. Streaming services such as YouTube, Netflix, and Amazon Prime are favored for watching videos, movies, and TV shows. Gaming, both online and offline, is also a significant activity. Educational apps and websites, especially those offering online courses and tutoring, have seen increased usage, with the COVID-19 pandemic accelerating the adoption of online learning. Messaging apps like WhatsApp and Telegram are primary tools for communication, enabling instant and constant connectivity with peers and family.

Increased online presence exposes teens to various risks, including cyberbullying, online predators, and misinformation. Awareness and education on safe internet practices are crucial. Excessive internet use, particularly social media, can affect teens' mental health, leading to issues such as anxiety, depression, and low self-esteem. While Indian teens are proficient in using digital devices, their understanding of digital literacy, including critical thinking and safe online practices, needs improvement.

Internet access varies across different socioeconomic backgrounds. Urban teens generally have better access compared to their rural counterparts, though this gap is narrowing. Parents play a significant role in shaping internet usage habits. In some cases, a lack of digital literacy among parents can lead to either over-regulation or insufficient guidance. Peer pressure significantly impacts how teens use the internet, from the platforms they join to the type of content they engage with and create.

Government initiatives like Digital India aim to increase internet accessibility and digital literacy across the country, particularly benefiting teens. Some schools have begun incorporating digital literacy into their curricula, teaching students about safe and responsible internet use.

Helping teens find a healthy balance between their online activities and offline responsibilities is a critical challenge. The internet offers vast opportunities for learning, skill development, and creativity. Encouraging positive and productive use of the Internet can lead to significant personal and academic growth.

Understanding the internet usage patterns of Indian teens is essential for addressing the unique challenges they face and leveraging the opportunities for their growth and development. By promoting digital literacy and safe online practices, we can help Indian teens navigate the digital world more securely and effectively.

CHAPTER VII

Popular Platforms and Apps

In today's digital age, social media and various online platforms have become integral parts of our daily lives, especially for teenagers. These platforms provide a plethora of opportunities for communication, entertainment, education, and self-expression. However, with the convenience and connectivity they offer, there also come significant challenges and risks. Understanding the popular platforms and apps that teens frequently use is essential for navigating the digital landscape safely and responsibly.

We delve into the most widely used social media networks, messaging apps, video streaming services, educational platforms, gaming platforms, and content creation tools. It highlights the unique features, benefits, and potential risks associated with each platform. By gaining insight into how these digital tools operate and their impact on users, you can make informed decisions about how to engage with them effectively and securely.

From the allure of Instagram and YouTube to the educational benefits of Khan Academy and Byju's, and the immersive experiences offered by gaming platforms like PUBG Mobile and Roblox, this chapter provides a comprehensive guide to the digital environments that shape the online experiences of Indian teens. As you explore the content, you will also find practical advice on maintaining digital safety and privacy, ensuring a positive and enriching online presence.

Social Media Platforms - Instagram is widely used by teens for sharing photos and short videos, with features like Stories, Reels, and IGTV being particularly popular. However, it poses risks such as cyberbullying, privacy concerns, and exposure to inappropriate content. Although Facebook is less popular among teens than it once was, it is still used for connecting with friends, joining groups, and accessing various content. The risks associated with Facebook include misinformation, privacy issues, and targeted advertising. Snapchat attracts teens with its disappearing messages, filters, and Stories, but it also comes with privacy concerns, potential for cyberbullying, and exposure to explicit content. TikTok is favored for creating and sharing short-form videos with a wide array of effects and music. Despite its popularity, TikTok can expose teens to inappropriate content, privacy issues, and potential addiction.

Messaging Apps - WhatsApp serves as the primary messaging app for text, voice, and video communication among teens, with group chats and status updates being widely used features. However, it is susceptible to the spread of misinformation, privacy concerns, and potential for cyberbullying. Telegram is used for secure messaging, large group chats, and channels for various interests, but it also poses privacy issues and exposure to illegal content or extremist groups. Discord is popular among gamers for voice, video, and text communication and is also used for community building around various interests. The risks include exposure to inappropriate content, cyberbullying, and potential addiction.

Video Streaming Platforms - YouTube is the go-to platform for teens to watch videos on a wide range of topics, including entertainment, education, and DIY tutorials. However, it also carries risks such as exposure to inappropriate content, misinformation, and privacy issues. Netflix is popular for streaming movies, TV shows, and documentaries, but it poses risks of potential addiction and exposure to mature content. Similarly, Amazon Prime Video is used for streaming a variety of movies, TV series, and original content, with risks similar to Netflix, including potential addiction and exposure to mature content.

Educational Platforms - Byju's is widely used for online learning, offering a variety of courses and interactive lessons, but it comes with data privacy concerns and the pressure of constant learning. Unacademy is popular for competitive exam preparation and educational courses, posing risks of data privacy issues and potential over-reliance on digital learning. Khan Academy is used for free educational resources covering a wide range of subjects, with minimal risks, although data privacy concerns remain.

Gaming Platforms - PUBG Mobile is extremely popular among teens for its battle royale gameplay, but it carries risks of addiction, exposure to violent content, and privacy concerns. Free Fire, another popular battle royale game, has similar risks of addiction and exposure to violent content. Roblox allows users to create and play games created by others, posing risks such as exposure to inappropriate content, privacy issues, and potential financial risks from in-game purchases.

Content Creation Platforms - YouTube is not only a viewing platform but also a popular content creation platform where many teens aspire to become YouTubers.

This comes with risks such as privacy concerns, exposure to online harassment, and the pressure of content creation. TikTok is favored for short, creative video content creation but poses risks of privacy issues, exposure to inappropriate content, and potential for cyberbullying. Instagram is used for sharing photos and videos, with many teens focusing on building a personal brand, which carries risks similar to YouTube and TikTok, along with added risks of social pressure and comparison.

Understanding the popular platforms and apps among Indian teens is crucial for addressing digital safety concerns. Each platform has unique benefits and risks, requiring tailored strategies to ensure a safe and positive online experience for teens. By promoting digital literacy and responsible usage, we can help teens navigate these platforms effectively.

CHAPTER VIII

Digital Literacy in Indian Schools

Digital literacy is the ability to effectively and responsibly use digital technologies for learning, communication, and everyday tasks. In India, the integration of digital literacy in schools is gaining importance, driven by the increasing role of technology in education and everyday life.

Current State of Digital Literacy - There is a significant disparity between urban and rural schools in terms of access to digital resources. Urban schools are generally better equipped with computers and internet connectivity, while rural schools often face challenges in these areas. While some schools have integrated digital literacy into their curriculum, many still lack comprehensive programs. Digital literacy is often taught as part of computer science or information technology courses. The effectiveness of digital literacy education depends heavily on the teachers' proficiency with digital tools. Many teachers, especially in rural areas, lack adequate training in digital technologies.

Key Components of Digital Literacy Education - Basic computer skills involve teaching students how to operate computers, use word processing software, and navigate the internet. These foundational skills are essential for students to participate in the digital world. Internet safety and cybersecurity education focuses on safe internet practices, recognizing cyber threats, and protecting personal information, helping students navigate the online world safely and responsibly. Digital communication training covers effective and respectful communication using digital tools, such as email, social media, and messaging apps, enhancing students' ability to collaborate and communicate in a digital environment. Research and information literacy involve teaching students how to find, evaluate, and use online information effectively and ethically, developing critical thinking skills and the ability to discern credible sources from misinformation. Digital creativity encourages students to use digital tools for creative expression, such as creating videos, graphics, and presentations, fostering innovation and the development of digital content creation skills. Coding and programming introduce students to basic coding and programming languages, preparing them for future careers in technology and enhancing problem-solving skills.

Challenges in Implementing Digital Literacy - Many schools, particularly in rural areas, lack the necessary infrastructure, such as computers, internet access, and electricity, to support digital literacy programs. A significant barrier is the lack of trained teachers who can effectively teach digital literacy, making continuous professional development essential. Developing a standardized digital literacy curriculum that is adaptable to different regions and schools remains a challenge. Limited financial resources hinder the ability to equip schools with the necessary technology and training programs.

Government Initiatives - The Digital India Campaign aims to provide universal digital literacy and bridge the digital divide by ensuring internet access and digital education in schools. Pradhan Mantri Gramin Digital Saksharta Abhiyan (PMGDISHA) focuses on making at least one person in every household digitally literate, which includes promoting digital literacy in schools. The SWAYAM and DIKSHA platforms provide free educational resources, including digital literacy courses for students and teachers.

Best Practices for Enhancing Digital Literacy - Public-private partnerships can help provide resources, training, and infrastructure to schools. Regular and comprehensive training programs for teachers are crucial to enhance their digital skills and teaching methods. Developing a digital literacy curriculum that is inclusive and adaptable to different learning environments and needs is essential. Community engagement involving parents and the community in digital literacy initiatives can reinforce learning and awareness. Regular assessment of digital literacy programs ensures they are effective and meet the needs of students.

Enhancing digital literacy in Indian schools is crucial for preparing students for a technology-driven future. By addressing the challenges and implementing best practices, schools can provide students with the skills and knowledge needed to thrive in the digital age.

Understanding Artificial Intelligence

CHAPTER IX

The AI Adventure of Samir and Priya

Samir and Priya, two high school students from Mumbai, are best friends who share a keen interest in technology. They have grown up in an era where artificial intelligence (AI) is becoming an integral part of everyday life, shaping their experiences in ways they are only beginning to understand.

As the new semester begins, Samir and Priya are excited to find out that their school has introduced a special course on Artificial Intelligence. Their teacher, Mr. Deshmukh, is enthusiastic about the subject and eager to introduce his students to the fascinating world of AI.

On the first day of the course, Mr. Deshmukh explains the basics of AI. He describes it as the simulation of human intelligence by machines, particularly computer systems. The students learn about different types of AI, including machine learning, natural language processing, and robotics.

Samir is particularly fascinated by machine learning, where algorithms enable computers to learn from and make predictions based on data. Priya, on the other hand, is intrigued by natural language processing, which allows machines to understand and respond to human language.

Mr. Deshmukh's classes reveal just how prevalent AI is in their daily lives. He points out that the voice assistants on their smartphones, like Google Assistant and Siri, are powered by AI. These assistants can understand spoken commands, answer questions, and even control smart home devices.

Samir and Priya start to notice AI everywhere. They realize that the recommendations they get on streaming services like Netflix and YouTube are driven by AI algorithms that analyze their viewing habits to suggest new content. Even the autocorrect feature on their phones and the spam filters in their email are examples of AI at work.

Inspired by their new knowledge, Samir and Priya decide to explore AI projects of their own. Samir, with his interest in machine learning, sets out to create a simple predictive model. He gathers data on his classmates' study habits and grades, and with some guidance from Mr. Deshmukh, builds a model that predicts how much time a student should study to achieve a certain grade.

Priya, meanwhile, decides to create a chatbot for their school's website. She designs the bot to answer common questions about school events, schedules, and facilities. Using natural language processing, the chatbot can understand and respond to students' queries in a conversational manner.

Both projects are a hit among their classmates. Samir's model becomes a fun tool for students to gauge their study plans, while Priya's chatbot makes it easier for students to find information quickly.

Through their projects and discussions in class, Samir and Priya also learn about the broader impact of AI on society. Mr. Deshmukh organizes a debate on the ethical implications of AI. The students discuss topics like privacy, data security, and the potential for job displacement due to automation.

Samir argues that while AI can lead to job losses in some sectors, it also creates new opportunities in tech and data analysis. Priya emphasizes the importance of ethical guidelines and regulations to ensure that AI is used responsibly and transparently.

They also explore how AI can be used for social good. For instance, they learn about AI applications in healthcare, such as early diagnosis of diseases and personalized treatment plans. They are inspired by stories of AI being used to predict natural disasters, improve agriculture, and even combat climate change.

As the course progresses, Samir and Priya become more passionate about AI. They start attending workshops and webinars, learning from experts in the field. They join online communities where they can share their projects and get feedback from other AI enthusiasts.

Their journey into the world of AI opens up new career aspirations. Samir dreams of becoming a data scientist, working on cutting-edge AI models. Priya envisions herself as a software engineer, developing AI-driven applications that solve real-world problems.

Samir and Priya's story is a testament to the transformative power of AI. Their curiosity and enthusiasm reflect the potential of young minds to harness technology for innovation and positive change. As they continue to explore AI, they are equipped with the knowledge and skills to navigate its complexities and contribute to its advancement.

Their journey underscores the importance of education in demystifying AI and empowering the next generation. Through hands-on projects, ethical discussions, and real-world applications, students like Samir and Priya are not just learning about AI; they are shaping the future with it.

As we delve deeper into this book, we will explore the intricacies of AI, its applications, and the critical role it plays in our digital landscape. By understanding AI, we can better navigate its opportunities and challenges, ensuring a safer and more innovative digital future for all.

CHAPTER X

What is AI?

Artificial Intelligence (AI) refers to the simulation of human intelligence processes by machines, especially computer systems. These processes include learning, which involves the acquisition of information and rules for using that information, reasoning, which uses rules to reach approximate or definite conclusions, and self-correction.

Key Concepts in AI - Machine Learning (ML) is a subset of AI that involves the use of algorithms and statistical models to enable computers to improve their performance on a task through experience. Examples of machine learning applications include email filtering, recommendation systems, and predictive text. Deep Learning, another subset of machine learning, uses neural networks with many layers, known as deep neural networks, to analyze various factors of data. Examples of deep learning applications include image recognition, speech recognition, and natural language processing.

Natural Language Processing (NLP) focuses on the interaction between computers and humans through natural language. Examples of NLP applications include language translation, sentiment analysis, and chatbots. Robotics is a branch of AI involving the design and creation of robots that can perform tasks autonomously or semi-autonomously, with examples including manufacturing robots, drones, and robotic vacuum cleaners. Computer Vision is a field of AI that enables computers to interpret and make decisions based on visual data from the world, with applications such as facial recognition, autonomous driving, and medical imaging analysis.

Applications of AI - In healthcare, AI is used for diagnostic tools, personalized medicine, and robotic surgeries, leading to improved accuracy in diagnoses, personalized treatment plans, and enhanced efficiency in medical procedures. In education, AI powers personalized learning platforms, grading systems, and educational chatbots, offering tailored learning experiences, efficient administrative tasks, and 24/7 student support. In finance, AI aids in fraud detection, algorithmic trading, and customer service automation, enhancing security, optimizing trading strategies, and improving customer interactions.

AI's impact on transportation includes autonomous vehicles, traffic management systems, and ride-sharing algorithms, which increase safety, reduce congestion, and improve efficiency in transportation services. In entertainment, AI is used for content recommendations, virtual reality (VR) experiences, and interactive gaming, providing personalized entertainment, immersive experiences, and innovative gaming environments. In retail, AI helps with inventory management, personalized shopping experiences, and automated customer service, leading to improved inventory accuracy, enhanced customer satisfaction, and efficient service delivery.

Benefits of AI - AI offers significant benefits, including efficiency and automation, as it can perform repetitive and mundane tasks quickly and accurately, freeing up human workers for more complex and creative work. It excels in data analysis and insights, as AI algorithms can analyze vast amounts of data to uncover patterns, trends, and insights that would be difficult for humans to detect. AI also enables personalization, tailoring products, services, and experiences to individual preferences, thus improving user satisfaction and engagement. Additionally, AI assists in decision-making by providing data-driven insights and recommendations.

Challenges and Ethical Considerations - Despite its benefits, AI presents challenges and ethical considerations. Bias and fairness are major concerns, as AI systems can inherit biases from their training data, leading to unfair and discriminatory outcomes. Ensuring fairness and equity in AI is a significant challenge. Privacy and security are also critical issues, as the use of AI involves the collection and analysis of vast amounts of data, raising concerns about data privacy and security. Job displacement is another concern, as the automation of tasks by AI can lead to job losses and require workers to adapt to new roles and skills. Accountability for decisions made by AI systems can be complex, especially in critical areas like healthcare and autonomous driving. Furthermore, transparency is a challenge, as AI systems, particularly those based on deep learning, can be opaque and difficult to interpret, making it challenging to understand how decisions are made.

Artificial Intelligence is a transformative technology with the potential to revolutionize various aspects of our lives. While it offers numerous benefits, it also presents challenges and ethical considerations that must be addressed to ensure that AI is developed and used responsibly. Understanding AI and its implications is essential for navigating the digital age effectively and responsibly.

CHAPTER XI

How AI is Integrated into Everyday Digital Tools

Artificial Intelligence (AI) has become an integral part of many digital tools that we use daily, enhancing their functionality and user experience. This section explores various everyday digital tools and how AI is embedded within them to make our lives more efficient and connected.

AI in Communication Tools - AI significantly enhances email services and messaging apps. For instance, AI algorithms in email services analyze incoming emails to detect and filter out spam, phishing attempts, and malware. Tools like Gmail use AI to suggest quick replies and even complete sentences as you type, making email communication faster. In messaging apps, AI-powered chatbots on platforms like Facebook Messenger and WhatsApp provide automated customer support, information, and services. Additionally, AI predicts the next word or phrase you're likely to type, enhancing typing efficiency and accuracy.

AI in Social Media Platforms - AI plays a crucial role in content recommendation, image and video recognition, and content moderation on social media platforms. Algorithms on platforms like Facebook, Instagram, and Twitter use AI to curate personalized news feeds based on user behavior and preferences. LinkedIn and other networks suggest connections based on mutual contacts, professional interests, and activity patterns. AI also automatically tags friends in photos, organizes media, and suggests relevant hashtags. Furthermore, AI helps identify and remove inappropriate or harmful content, maintaining platform safety and user experience.

AI in Search Engines and Browsers - Search engines and browsers leverage AI to deliver personalized search results and targeted ads. Google and other search engines use AI to provide personalized search results based on user history, location, and preferences. AI-driven voice recognition technology enables voice search functionality, making information retrieval hands-free and convenient. AI also analyzes user data to serve relevant ads, improving the effectiveness of advertising campaigns.

AI in Entertainment and Media - AI enhances streaming services and content creation in the entertainment and media industry. Platforms like Netflix, Amazon Prime, and YouTube use AI to recommend shows, movies, and videos based on viewing history and preferences. Music services like Spotify create personalized playlists and suggest new music using AI. Additionally, AI tools assist in editing videos and photos, applying effects, and even generating content such as music and artwork.

AI in E-commerce - E-commerce platforms use AI for personalized shopping, dynamic pricing, and customer service. AI algorithms on platforms like Amazon and Flipkart suggest products based on browsing history, past purchases, and user preferences. AI adjusts prices in real-time based on demand, competition, and user behavior.

Furthermore, AI chatbots provide instant customer support, handle inquiries, and resolve issues without human intervention.

AI in Smart Devices - AI integration in smart devices enhances functionality and user experience. In smartphones, AI-powered assistants like Siri, Google Assistant, and Alexa perform tasks, answer questions, and control smart home devices. AI improves photo quality, provides real-time translation, and recognizes scenes and objects. In smart home devices, AI enables home automation, learning user habits and optimizing settings for comfort and energy efficiency. Wearables use AI to analyze physical activity, monitor health metrics, and provide personalized health insights.

AI in Productivity Tools - AI improves productivity tools like office suites and project management software. AI tools like Grammarly offer writing assistance, grammar checking, and style suggestions. Excel and other spreadsheet software use AI to automate data analysis, generate insights, and create visualizations. In project management tools like Trello and Asana, AI helps automate repetitive tasks, schedule, and prioritize work.

AI's integration into everyday digital tools has significantly enhanced their capabilities, making them more intuitive, efficient, and user-friendly. As AI technology continues to evolve, its role in our daily digital interactions will only grow, providing even greater benefits and transforming how we live and work. Understanding these integrations helps us better navigate and leverage these tools for maximum advantage.

CHAPTER XII

The Role of AI in Social Media and Gaming

Artificial Intelligence (AI) has revolutionized various aspects of our digital lives, particularly in social media and gaming. As AI technologies continue to advance, their integration into these platforms has profoundly transformed how we interact, communicate, and entertain ourselves online. AI not only enhances user experiences but also introduces new challenges and ethical considerations.

From curating personalized content and moderating harmful posts to creating intelligent, adaptive game environments and enhancing player engagement, AI is at the forefront of these digital transformations. Understanding how AI operates within these platforms helps users navigate the digital world more effectively and safely.

We will delve into the ways AI personalizes social media feeds, targets advertisements, and uses image and video recognition to organize content. In gaming, we examine how AI generates dynamic game worlds, creates realistic non-player characters (NPCs), and analyzes player behavior to offer tailored experiences. Additionally, we will discuss the potential risks and ethical implications of AI in these domains, such as data privacy concerns, algorithmic biases, and the impact on mental health.

By gaining a deeper understanding of the role of AI in social media and gaming, you will be better equipped to leverage these technologies to enhance your digital experiences while remaining aware of the potential pitfalls. This chapter aims to provide a comprehensive overview of AI's transformative impact on the platforms that dominate our online lives.

AI in Social Media - AI significantly enhances social media platforms by personalizing content, moderating harmful material, boosting user engagement, and improving image and video recognition. AI algorithms analyze user behavior, preferences, and interactions to curate personalized news feeds on platforms like Facebook, Instagram, and Twitter, ensuring users see content most relevant and engaging to them. Additionally, AI analyzes user data to deliver targeted advertisements, increasing the relevance of ads shown to users and improving engagement rates for advertisers.

Content moderation is another critical area where AI excels. AI systems automatically detect and flag harmful or inappropriate content, such as hate speech, violence, and explicit material, helping maintain a safer and more respectful online environment. AI tools also identify and reduce the spread of misinformation by flagging or removing false content and providing fact-checking resources.

User engagement is significantly enhanced through AI-powered chatbots, which interact with users, provide customer support, and facilitate transactions. These bots can answer questions, provide recommendations, and enhance user engagement. Moreover, AI suggests relevant content, groups, and connections based on user behavior and interests, keeping users engaged and encouraging the discovery of new content.

In the realm of image and video recognition, AI technologies like facial recognition automatically tag people in photos and organize media, making it easier for users to manage and share their content. AI also applies filters, effects, and edits to photos and videos, enhancing the quality and appeal of user-generated content.

AI in Gaming -AI's impact on gaming is profound, enhancing gameplay, generating procedural content, analyzing player behavior, and supporting virtual and augmented reality experiences. AI creates intelligent, adaptive opponents that learn and evolve based on the player's actions, providing a more challenging and engaging experience. AI algorithms also adjust the difficulty level in real-time based on the player's skill and progress, ensuring a balanced and enjoyable gaming experience.

Procedural content generation is another area where AI shines. AI generates diverse and complex game environments, levels, and scenarios dynamically, providing unique experiences for each playthrough. It also assists in creating diverse and realistic non-player characters (NPCs) with unique behaviors and personalities, enriching the game's narrative and immersion.

AI analyzes player behavior, preferences, and playstyles to offer personalized recommendations, such as new games, in-game items, and tailored content. It also monitors player behavior to detect cheating and unfair practices, ensuring a fair gaming environment for all players.

In virtual reality (VR) and augmented reality (AR), AI enhances experiences by providing realistic interactions, environments, and scenarios that adapt to the user's actions and preferences. AI interprets user gestures and voice commands to provide more intuitive and immersive control mechanisms in VR and AR games.

AI also plays a crucial role in game development. AI tools assist game developers in creating and refining game elements, such as textures, animations, and storylines, streamlining the development process and enhancing creativity. Furthermore, AI automates testing and quality assurance processes, identifying bugs and performance issues more efficiently than manual testing.

AI plays a pivotal role in enhancing both social media and gaming experiences. In social media, AI improves content personalization, moderates harmful content, and boosts user engagement. In gaming, AI enhances gameplay, generates dynamic content, analyzes player behavior, and aids in game development. As AI technology continues to advance, its impact on social media and gaming will grow, providing more sophisticated, engaging, and safe experiences for users.

Understanding Deepfakes

CHAPTER XIII

Priya and the Fake Video

Priya, a 15-year-old student from Mumbai, was known for her creativity and tech-savviness. She loved making videos and was an active member of her school's media club. Her dream was to become a filmmaker, and she spent her free time experimenting with different video editing software. Little did she know that her passion for videos would lead her to a deeper understanding of a new digital threat: deepfakes.

One day, during lunch break, Priya and her friends were huddled around a phone, watching a viral video. The video showed a popular Bollywood actor saying some controversial things about his co-stars. Priya found it odd because she had seen an interview with the same actor the previous day, where he seemed friendly and respectful.

Her friends were quick to believe the video, but Priya's instincts told her something was off. She decided to investigate further.

Priya started by analyzing the video closely. She noticed small inconsistencies in the actor's facial expressions and the way his mouth moved while speaking. She remembered reading about deepfakes, a technology that uses AI to create realistic fake videos, and began to suspect that this might be one.

After school, Priya went home and searched for more information about deepfakes. She learned that deepfakes use deep learning algorithms to superimpose one person's face onto another's body, creating realistic but fake videos. These videos could be used to spread false information, manipulate opinions, and damage reputations.

The next day, Priya approached her teacher, Mr. Singh, with her findings. She suggested that they should educate the students about deepfakes and how to identify them. Mr. Singh agreed and decided to make it a class project.

The class was divided into groups, and each group was assigned a task related to deepfakes. Priya's group was responsible for explaining the technology behind deepfakes and demonstrating how to spot them. Other groups worked on the history of deepfakes, real-life examples, and the ethical implications.

Priya and her group spent days researching and preparing their presentation. They discovered various tools and techniques used to create deepfakes, such as GANs (Generative Adversarial Networks) and autoencoders. They also learned about telltale signs of deepfakes, like unnatural eye movements, mismatched lighting, and inconsistent lip-syncing.

When the day of the presentation arrived, Priya's group demonstrated how a deepfake video is made using freely available software. They showed the class how easy it was to create a convincing fake video and highlighted the importance of being skeptical about what they see online.

A Real-Life Impact

During the Q&A session, a student named Anjali shared her experience of almost falling for a deepfake video. She had received a video of her favorite singer promoting a fake charity. Thanks to Priya's presentation, she realized the signs and decided to verify the information before donating.

Priya's efforts not only educated her classmates but also empowered them to be more vigilant about the content they consume online. The project was a huge success, and the school decided to include a workshop on digital literacy and deepfakes as part of their curriculum.

Priya's story illustrates the importance of understanding deepfakes in today's digital age. Her curiosity and determination led to a valuable lesson for her entire school community, highlighting the need for awareness and critical thinking when it comes to digital content.

As we explore this chapter, we will delve deeper into the world of deepfakes. By understanding how they work and learning to identify them, we can protect ourselves from misinformation and maintain the integrity of the digital space, just like Priya and her friends.

CHAPTER XIV

What are Deepfakes?

In the rapidly evolving digital landscape, deepfake technology has emerged as one of the most intriguing and potentially disruptive innovations. Deepfakes leverage the power of Artificial Intelligence (AI) to create hyper-realistic but fake videos and images. This technology has the ability to manipulate visual and audio content in ways that can convincingly mimic real people, making it increasingly difficult to distinguish between genuine and fabricated media.

Definition and Origins - Deepfake is a portmanteau of "deep learning" and "fake." Deep learning, a subset of AI, involves neural networks with many layers that can learn and make intelligent decisions independently. Deepfake technology uses these neural networks to analyze and replicate patterns in audio and visual data, allowing for the creation of highly realistic simulations. The origins of deepfake technology can be traced back to advances in computer graphics and AI research. Initially, these techniques were developed for benign purposes such as improving computer-generated imagery (CGI) in movies and video games. However, it soon became apparent that the same technology could be used to manipulate media for more nefarious purposes.

How Deepfakes Work - Creating a deepfake typically involves several steps. First, a large dataset of the target's images or videos is collected, providing the training material for the AI model. Then, a deep learning algorithm, often a type of neural network known as a Generative Adversarial Network (GAN), is trained on the dataset. GANs consist of two parts: a generator that creates fake content and a discriminator that evaluates the authenticity of the content.

The two parts work together in a loop, with the generator improving its output based on the discriminator's feedback until the fake content is indistinguishable from real content. Finally, once trained, the model can generate new images or videos that mimic the appearance and movements of the target, including swapping faces in videos, altering speech, and creating entirely new sequences of actions or words that the person never performed or said.

Applications and Misuse - While deepfakes have legitimate applications in entertainment and education, their potential for misuse is a significant concern. In entertainment and art, deepfakes can be used to create special effects in movies, generate realistic avatars in video games, and produce creative content in the arts. In education and training, they can simulate realistic scenarios for training purposes, such as medical procedures, flight simulations, and historical reenactments. However, deepfakes can also be used to create false videos of public figures, spreading misinformation and manipulating public opinion, targeting individuals with fake videos that harm their reputation or cause emotional distress, and impersonating individuals for fraudulent activities, such as bypassing biometric security systems.

Recognizing and Combating Deepfakes - Identifying

deepfakes can be challenging, but certain signs may indicate a video or image is manipulated. Look for inconsistencies in facial expressions, blinking, or movements that seem unnatural or exaggerated, mismatched lighting and shadows that do not align with the environment, whether the mouth movements match the spoken words accurately, and blurry edges, especially around the face and hair, or any visual artifacts that suggest tampering. Combating the threat of deepfakes requires a multi-faceted approach.

Technological solutions involve advances in AI and machine learning to develop tools that can detect deepfakes by analyzing subtle inconsistencies and patterns. Regulation and legislation are being developed by governments and regulatory bodies to address the challenges posed by deepfakes through legislation aimed at penalizing malicious use and protecting individuals' rights. Increasing public awareness about deepfakes and educating people on how to recognize them is crucial, and media literacy programs can equip individuals with the skills to critically evaluate the content they encounter online. Social media platforms and content providers also need to take proactive measures to identify and remove deepfake content that violates their policies.

Deepfake technology represents a powerful tool with the potential for both positive and negative impacts. Understanding what deepfakes are, how they work, and their potential applications and misuses is the first step in safeguarding against their negative effects. By staying informed and adopting a proactive approach to digital literacy and cybersecurity, we can better navigate the challenges posed by this advanced technology and protect the integrity of our digital experiences.

CHAPTER XV

How Deepfakes are Integrated into Everyday Digital Tools

Deepfake technology, initially perceived as a novelty or niche application of artificial intelligence, has quickly found its way into everyday digital tools, reshaping various aspects of media, communication, and entertainment. Understanding how deepfakes are embedded in these tools is essential for recognizing both their potential benefits and associated risks.

Integration of Deepfakes in Digital Tools - Deepfake technology is widely used in social media and communication platforms. Face-swapping filters on apps like Snapchat and Instagram utilize deepfake technology to replace users' faces with those of celebrities or fictional characters, providing entertainment and demonstrating real-time facial manipulation capabilities. Additionally, deepfakes enhance augmented reality (AR) effects in apps, allowing users to apply filters that significantly alter their appearance, such as changing their age, gender, or transforming them into animals or mythical creatures.

In video editing and production, deepfake technology has also made significant inroads. Apps like Reface and Zao enable users to superimpose their faces onto famous movie scenes or music videos, making it easy to create convincing deepfake videos with minimal effort. Professional editing software, such as Adobe After Effects and Premiere Pro, is beginning to incorporate AI-based tools that leverage deepfake technology for tasks like automated video editing, enhancing low-quality footage, or creating digital doubles for actors.

The entertainment and gaming industries have embraced deepfake technology as well. Realistic avatars in video games and virtual worlds are created using deepfakes to mimic the facial expressions and movements of players, enhancing user experience in games like The Sims and custom character creators in various RPGs. Additionally, virtual influencers, digital characters that look and behave like real people, are being used increasingly in marketing and social media to engage with audiences.

Educational and training tools are also benefiting from deepfake technology. Interactive learning experiences are enhanced by deepfakes, allowing educational platforms to create immersive scenarios, such as history lessons featuring AI-generated versions of historical figures. In simulation training, deepfakes provide realistic scenarios for effective learning, such as in flight simulators or medical training where trainees interact with highly realistic virtual patients or practice emergency procedures.

Customer service and virtual assistants are another area where deepfakes are making an impact. Virtual assistants like Siri, Alexa, and Google Assistant are incorporating deepfake-generated voices and faces to offer more human-like interactions, making conversations with AI feel more natural and engaging. Companies are also using deepfake technology to create realistic customer service avatars that handle inquiries visually and verbally, providing a personalized customer service experience.

In the realm of content creation and media, deepfakes are being used in innovative ways. News organizations are experimenting with AI-generated news anchors that can present news 24/7 without human intervention, using deepfake technology to mimic the appearance and speech of real anchors. Additionally, synthetic media created by deepfakes is enabling automated content creation, especially in marketing and entertainment, where entire articles, images, or videos are generated by AI.

Benefits and Risks

The benefits of integrating deepfake technology into digital tools are numerous. It enhances creativity by providing new tools for content creation, entertainment, and artistic expression. Deepfakes also democratize content creation, allowing individuals without technical skills to produce high-quality media. In education and training, deepfakes provide interactive and immersive experiences that can improve understanding and retention.

However, the risks associated with deepfake technology are significant. The ability to create highly realistic fake content can be misused to spread misinformation, commit fraud, or manipulate public opinion. Deepfakes can also infringe on privacy by creating unauthorized or harmful representations of individuals, potentially damaging reputations. Moreover, the use of deepfake technology raises ethical and legal questions regarding consent, authenticity, and accountability.

The integration of deepfake technology into everyday digital tools offers exciting possibilities for creativity, personalization, and enhanced user experiences. However, it also introduces significant risks related to misinformation, privacy, and ethical use. By understanding how deepfakes are embedded in various digital tools, we can better appreciate their potential while remaining vigilant about their misuse. As this technology continues to evolve, it is crucial for users, developers, and policymakers to work together to harness its benefits responsibly and mitigate its risks.

CHAPTER XVI

The Role of Deepfakes in Digital Space & Social Media

Deepfakes, utilizing artificial intelligence (AI) to create hyper-realistic but fabricated images, videos, and audio, have become a significant force in the digital space and social media. These technologies open new avenues for creativity and innovation but also pose substantial risks, particularly in terms of misinformation and privacy invasion. This section explores the multifaceted role of deepfakes in digital space and social media, highlighting both their positive applications and potential dangers.

Positive Applications of Deepfakes - In the entertainment and creative arts, deepfakes allow filmmakers to create stunning visual effects, de-age actors, or even bring deceased actors back to life for new performances. For example, the technology was used to create a younger version of Mark Hamill's Luke Skywalker in "The Mandalorian." Artists and marketers use deepfakes to produce engaging content in music videos and advertising, featuring realistic digital avatars and using well-known faces without requiring the actual presence of the celebrities.

In education and training, deepfake technology helps create lifelike reenactments of historical events, allowing students to interact with historical figures in a way that brings history to life. It also enables realistic language practice scenarios, where students can have conversations with AI-generated avatars that respond naturally. Companies deploy virtual assistants and customer service avatars that use deepfake technology to provide a more personalized and human-like interaction, improving user experience and satisfaction. Deepfakes are also used to create personalized advertisements that directly address individual consumers, making marketing campaigns more effective and engaging, and influencers and brands generate unique and eye-catching content that stands out on crowded social media platforms.

Risks and Challenges - However, deepfakes also present significant risks. They can be used to create convincing fake news videos that spread misinformation and manipulate public opinion, with significant implications for politics and elections, where fabricated videos can influence voter behavior. Malicious actors use deepfakes to create social media posts that incite unrest, spread false narratives, or damage reputations. Deepfakes can be used to create non-consensual explicit content, often targeting women, leading to severe psychological harm and reputational damage. Cybercriminals use deepfake technology to impersonate individuals, bypass security systems, and commit fraud. The prevalence of deepfakes can erode public trust in digital content, making it difficult for people to distinguish between real and fake media, undermining legitimate news sources and social media platforms. As deepfakes become more sophisticated, traditional methods of verifying authenticity, such as reverse image searches and manual inspection, become less effective.

Combating the Negative Impact of Deepfakes - Combating the negative impact of deepfakes requires a multi-faceted approach. Technological solutions, such as AI-based tools, are being developed to detect deepfakes by analyzing inconsistencies and subtle artifacts that are often present in manipulated media. Blockchain and digital watermarking technologies can help verify the authenticity of digital content by providing an immutable record of its origin and alterations. Governments are starting to introduce laws to criminalize the malicious use of deepfakes, such as non-consensual explicit content and political misinformation, and establishing regulatory bodies to oversee the use of deepfake technology and enforce compliance with legal standards. Public awareness and education are crucial, with media literacy programs teaching individuals how to critically evaluate digital content and recognize deepfakes, and social media platforms and governments running awareness campaigns to inform users about the risks of deepfakes and how to protect themselves. Social media platforms need robust content moderation policies that include measures to detect and remove deepfakes that violate community guidelines, and platforms should be transparent about the methods they use to detect deepfakes and provide users with the ability to report suspected deepfake content.

Deepfakes represent a powerful and rapidly evolving technology with significant implications for the digital space and social media. While they offer exciting possibilities for creativity and innovation, they also pose serious risks that need to be addressed. By leveraging technological solutions, enacting robust legal frameworks, promoting public awareness, and holding digital platforms accountable, we can harness the positive potential of deepfakes while mitigating their negative impacts. Understanding and navigating the complex role of deepfakes in the digital era is crucial for ensuring a safer and more trustworthy online environment.

Privacy and Data Protection

The Privacy Awakening of Aarav and Neha

Aarav and Neha, two tech-savvy high school students from Bengaluru, are known among their friends as the go-to experts for anything digital. They both enjoy exploring the latest apps, social media platforms, and online games. However, their understanding of privacy and data protection is about to take a significant leap forward.

One day in their computer science class, their teacher, Ms. Rao, announces a special guest lecture on privacy and data protection. The guest speaker is Mr. Krishnan, a cybersecurity expert who works with various tech companies to secure their data.

Mr. Krishnan starts his lecture with a simple question: "How many of you have read the terms and conditions before signing up for a new app or service?" Aarav and Neha, along with their classmates, look at each other and realize none of them have ever bothered to read the fine print.

Mr. Krishnan explains how most apps and websites collect data, often without users fully understanding what they are agreeing to. He talks about the types of data collected, from basic information like names and email addresses to more sensitive data like location, browsing history, and even personal preferences.

He shares a startling example: "Imagine a social media app that collects your location data every few minutes. It knows where you go, how long you stay, and can even predict your daily routine." Aarav and Neha are shocked to realize how much information their favorite apps might be collecting.

To drive the point home, Ms. Rao assigns a project for the class: each student must request a data download from one of their social media accounts and analyze what data has been collected. Aarav chooses Facebook, while Neha opts for Instagram.

When Aarav receives his data file, he is stunned by its size. It contains every post he has ever made, every comment, every like, and detailed logs of his interactions. There are also logs of his location history and metadata from photos he has uploaded.

Neha's Instagram data is equally revealing. It includes her entire search history, lists of people she interacts with most frequently, and even a record of how much time she spends on the app each day.

The Impact of Data Sharing

As Aarav and Neha dig deeper, they realize the potential consequences of data sharing. Mr. Krishnan explains how companies use this data for targeted advertising. "When you see an ad for something you were just talking about, that's no coincidence. It's data at work," he says.

Aarav recalls an incident where he and his friends were discussing a new smartphone, and later that day, he saw ads for that very phone on multiple websites. It suddenly makes sense.

Steps to Protect Personal Information

Determined to take control of their digital footprints, Aarav and Neha follow Mr. Krishnan's advice on protecting their personal information. They start by adjusting their privacy settings on social media, limiting who can see their posts and who has access to their location data.

They also begin using stronger, unique passwords for each of their accounts and enable two-factor authentication wherever possible. Aarav discovers a password manager app that helps him keep track of his numerous passwords securely.

Empowered by their newfound understanding, Aarav and Neha decide to share their knowledge with their peers. They organize a workshop at school, demonstrating how to adjust privacy settings on popular apps, the importance of strong passwords, and how to recognize phishing attempts.

Their classmates are amazed by how much they didn't know about privacy and data protection. Neha explains, "It's not just about keeping our information safe from hackers; it's about understanding how our data is used and making informed choices."

The Bigger Picture

Mr. Krishnan returns for another session, this time discussing the broader implications of data privacy. He talks about data breaches, where even large corporations can fall victim to cyber-attacks, exposing millions of users' personal information.

He also covers the ethical considerations of data collection, stressing the need for regulations that protect users' privacy. Aarav and Neha learn about India's Data Protection Bill, which aims to give citizens more control over their personal data.

Aarav and Neha's journey into the world of privacy and data protection is eye-opening. They realize that while technology offers incredible convenience and opportunities, it also comes with risks that must be managed responsibly.

Their story highlights the importance of digital literacy, not just in using technology but in understanding its implications. By taking proactive steps to protect their personal information, Aarav and Neha set an example for their peers, demonstrating that privacy is a fundamental right in the digital age.

As we delve further into this chapter, we will explore practical strategies and tips for protecting personal data, the role of laws and regulations, and the ethical dimensions of data privacy. Understanding these aspects is crucial for navigating the digital world safely and responsibly.

CHAPTER XVIII

The Importance of Data Privacy

Data privacy refers to the proper handling, processing, storage, and protection of personal information. In an age where digital activities are integral to daily life, understanding and maintaining data privacy is crucial. For teens, who are increasingly active online, protecting their personal information is vital to safeguarding their well-being and future opportunities.

Key Aspects of Data Privacy - Personal information includes any data that can be used to identify an individual, such as names, addresses, phone numbers, email addresses, and social media profiles. Examples of personal information include school records, medical history, browsing habits, and online purchases. Various entities collect personal data, including social media platforms, e-commerce sites, educational institutions, and mobile apps. This data is often used for targeted advertising, improving services, conducting research, and enhancing user experiences.

Why Data Privacy Matters - Protecting personal information is essential for preventing identity theft. Personal information can be stolen and used for fraudulent activities, such as opening bank accounts, applying for credit cards, or making unauthorized purchases. Safeguarding personal information reduces the risk of identity theft and associated financial and legal complications. Data privacy also helps safeguard personal security. Unauthorized access to personal data can lead to stalking, harassment, and physical threats. Ensuring data privacy helps protect individuals from security breaches and personal harm.

Maintaining control over personal information is another crucial aspect of data privacy. Without proper data privacy, individuals lose control over who has access to their information and how it is used. Data privacy practices ensure that individuals can control their personal information and consent to its use. Protecting one's digital footprint is also important. A digital footprint includes all traces of an individual's online activity. A lack of privacy can lead to a permanent and publicly accessible record of actions, opinions, and behaviors. Managing data privacy helps maintain a positive digital footprint, which is crucial for future opportunities, such as college admissions and job prospects.

Compliance with legal regulations is a vital component of data privacy. Violating data privacy regulations can lead to legal consequences for both individuals and organizations. Understanding and adhering to data privacy laws, such as the General Data Protection Regulation (GDPR) and India's Personal Data Protection Bill, ensures legal compliance and protection of rights.

Best Practices for Ensuring Data Privacy - Implementing strong passwords and authentication, such as using complex passwords and enabling two-factor authentication, protects accounts from unauthorized access. Regularly reviewing and adjusting privacy settings on social media platforms, mobile apps, and online services limits the amount of personal information shared publicly and controls who can view it. Using encryption tools to protect sensitive data stored on devices and transmitted online ensures that data remains secure and unreadable to unauthorized parties.

Staying informed about the latest data privacy threats and best practices empowers individuals to make informed decisions and adopt safe online behaviors. Participating in educational programs and workshops increases awareness and knowledge about data privacy. Regular monitoring of accounts and online activities for any unusual or unauthorized actions allows for early detection of potential breaches and timely intervention. Using secure and trusted Wi-Fi networks and avoiding public Wi-Fi for sensitive transactions reduces the risk of data interception by unauthorized users.

Data privacy is essential for protecting personal information, ensuring personal security, maintaining control over one's digital footprint, and complying with legal regulations. By adopting best practices and staying informed about potential threats, teens can safeguard their data and enjoy a safer and more secure online experience. Understanding the importance of data privacy empowers individuals to take proactive steps in protecting their digital lives.

CHAPTER XIX

How Data is Collected and Used

In the digital age, data collection has become ubiquitous, with various entities gathering information about users' online and offline activities. Understanding how data is collected and used is essential for maintaining privacy and making informed decisions about sharing personal information.

Methods of Data Collection - Data collection occurs through direct and automated means, as well as third-party sources and IoT devices. Direct collection involves data provided directly by users through forms, surveys, account registrations, and online purchases. Examples include names, email addresses, phone numbers, mailing addresses, and payment information. Automated collection methods include cookies, small text files stored on users' devices by websites to track browsing activity and preferences, web beacons, tiny invisible graphics embedded in emails or web pages to monitor user behavior, IP address tracking to identify and track users' location and online activity, and device fingerprinting, which collects information about a device's characteristics to uniquely identify and track it/

Third-party collection involves data gathered by social media platforms, advertising networks, and data brokers. Social media interactions, likes, shares, and comments are examples of data collected by social media platforms, while advertising networks gather data to build user profiles and deliver targeted advertisements. Data brokers collect and sell personal information from various sources such as public records, online purchases, and social media activity. Sensors and IoT devices like smart home devices, wearables, and other IoT devices also collect data. Examples include fitness trackers, smart thermostats, and voice-activated assistants.

Types of Data Collected - The types of data collected include personal identification information (PII), behavioral data, demographic data, location data, and health and fitness data. Personal identification information includes names, addresses, phone numbers, email addresses, and social security numbers, used for account creation, customer service, and personalized communication. Behavioral data encompasses browsing history, search queries, click patterns, and online purchase history, used to analyze user behavior, improve website functionality, and deliver personalized content and advertisements.

Demographic data includes age, gender, income level, education, and occupation, used for market research, audience segmentation, and targeted marketing campaigns. Location data, such as GPS coordinates, IP address location, and location-based service usage, is used for location-based services, local advertising, and tracking user movement patterns. Health and fitness data, including activity levels, heart rate, sleep patterns, and dietary habits, are used by fitness apps and health monitoring devices to provide personalized health insights and recommendations.

How Data is Used - Data is used for personalization and user experience, marketing and advertising, product and service improvement, research and development, and security and fraud prevention. In personalization and user experience, data is used to deliver customized content, recommendations, and advertisements based on user preferences and behavior. Examples include streaming services suggesting shows, e-commerce sites recommending products, and social media platforms curating news feeds. In marketing and advertising, data is used to deliver personalized ads to specific audiences and for behavioral retargeting, showing ads to users who have previously interacted with a website or product. Examples include Facebook ads based on user interests, Google AdWords targeting search queries, and email marketing campaigns. Data is also used for product and service improvement through data analytics, identifying trends, preferences, and areas for improvement, and A/B testing, comparing different versions of a product or service to determine which performs better.

Examples include improving app functionality, enhancing user interfaces, and optimizing website performance. In research and development, data is used for market research, understanding market trends, consumer behavior, and the competitive landscape, and product innovation, developing new products and features based on user needs and preferences. Examples include tech companies innovating based on user feedback, academic research using anonymized data, and healthcare advancements from patient data. Data is used for security and fraud prevention through anomaly detection, identifying unusual patterns to prevent fraudulent activities, and user authentication, verifying user identity through data analysis and machine learning algorithms. Examples include banks monitoring transactions for fraud, online services using multi-factor authentication, and cybersecurity firms analyzing threat data.

Ethical Considerations and Privacy Concerns - Ethical considerations and privacy concerns include informed consent, data security, data minimization, and accountability and compliance. Informed consent involves ensuring users are aware of what data is being collected and how it will be used, with opt-in/opt-out options allowing users to consent to or decline data collection. Examples include clear privacy policies, cookie consent banners, and user settings for data sharing. Data security involves implementing strong security practices to protect collected data from breaches and unauthorized access, with encryption used to safeguard data during transmission and storage. Examples include secure websites (HTTPS), encrypted databases, and regular security audits. Data minimization involves collecting only the data necessary for a specific purpose and avoiding excessive data collection.

Examples include minimizing personal data in forms, anonymizing data where possible, and regularly reviewing data retention policies. Accountability and compliance involve adhering to data protection laws and regulations, such as the General Data Protection Regulation (GDPR) and India's Personal Data Protection Bill, and adopting ethical data collection and usage practices to build user trust. Examples include conducting data protection impact assessments, appointing data protection officers, and implementing user rights management.

Understanding how data is collected and used is crucial for maintaining privacy and making informed decisions about personal information. By being aware of the methods and purposes of data collection, users can take steps to protect their privacy and engage with digital services more securely and confidently. Ethical considerations and privacy concerns must be addressed to ensure that data collection practices respect user rights and foster trust in the digital ecosystem.

CHAPTER XX

Steps to Protect Personal Information

Protecting personal information is essential to safeguarding privacy and preventing identity theft, cyber-attacks, and other forms of digital exploitation. Here are practical steps you can take to protect your personal information online.

Use Strong and Unique Passwords - Creating complex passwords using a mix of letters (both uppercase and lowercase), numbers, and special characters is crucial. Avoid common passwords like "password123" or "123456." Additionally, using different passwords for different accounts can prevent a breach on one site from compromising others.

Enable Two-Factor Authentication (2FA) - Adding an extra layer of security by enabling 2FA on your accounts is highly recommended. This requires a second form of verification, such as a code sent to your phone, in addition to your password. Using authenticator apps like Google Authenticator or Authy for generating verification codes is more secure than relying on SMS, which can be intercepted.

Be Cautious with Personal Information - Limiting the sharing of personal information and avoiding oversharing on social media is important. Regularly reviewing and adjusting privacy settings on social media and other online accounts can help control who can see your information.

Monitor Accounts Regularly - Regularly reviewing bank

and credit card statements for any unauthorized transactions is a good practice. Setting up account alerts to receive notifications of any suspicious activity can also help you stay on top of your account security.

Use Secure Connections - Avoid using public Wi-Fi for sensitive transactions like online banking. If you need to access the internet in public places, using a Virtual Private Network (VPN) is a safer option. Additionally, ensuring websites use HTTPS (indicated by a padlock symbol in the address bar) before entering any personal information is crucial.

Be Wary of Phishing Scams - Being cautious of emails, messages, or websites that ask for personal information is essential. Always verify the source before clicking on links or providing information. Checking the sender's email address for signs of phishing, such as misspellings or unfamiliar domains, can also help prevent scams.

Keep Software Updated - Regularly updating your operating system, browsers, and apps with the latest security patches and updates is important. Using antivirus and anti-malware software and ensuring they are regularly updated can protect against threats.

Encrypt Sensitive Data - Using encryption tools to encrypt sensitive files on your devices and backup drives can protect them from unauthorized access. For secure communication, using encrypted messaging apps like Signal or WhatsApp is recommended.

Manage Social Media Privacy - Reviewing and adjusting

privacy settings on social media platforms to control who can see your posts and personal information is necessary. Being selective with friend requests and follow requests by only accepting those from people you know and trust can also enhance your privacy.

Educate Yourself and Stay Informed - Regularly educating yourself about new security threats and best practices for protecting personal information is crucial. Being skeptical of unknown links and downloads and avoiding clicking on unknown links or downloading files from untrusted sources can also help protect your information.

Protecting personal information requires vigilance and proactive measures. By implementing these steps, you can significantly enhance your online security and reduce the risk of your personal information being compromised. Regularly reviewing and updating your security practices is essential to staying ahead of potential threats in the digital landscape.

Social Media Safety

CHAPTER XXI

The Social Media Journey of Riya and Ankit

Riya and Ankit, two friends from Hyderabad, are typical teenagers who enjoy spending their free time on social media. They use platforms like Instagram, Facebook, and Snapchat to stay connected with friends, share moments, and follow their favorite celebrities. However, their journey into the world of social media safety is about to teach them valuable lessons.

Riya loves taking photos and often posts them on Instagram, while Ankit enjoys making funny videos and sharing them on TikTok. They both enjoy the likes, comments, and attention their posts receive. Social media feels like a fun, virtual extension of their social lives.

One day, Riya receives a friend request from someone she doesn't know. The profile picture looks friendly enough, and they have a few mutual friends, so she accepts the request without much thought. The new friend starts liking all her photos and commenting on her posts. Initially, Riya is flattered by the attention.

However, things soon take a troubling turn. The person starts sending her private messages, asking personal questions and making her feel uncomfortable. Riya doesn't know how to handle it and confides in Ankit, who urges her to talk to their school counselor, Ms. Sharma.

Ms. Sharma listens to Riya's story and commends her for speaking up. She explains the importance of privacy settings on social media platforms. Together, they go through Riya's Instagram account, adjusting her settings to ensure only her real friends can see her posts and contact her directly.

Ms. Sharma also introduces Riya and Ankit to the concept of "stranger danger" in the digital world. Just like they wouldn't trust a stranger on the street, they should be cautious about who they interact with online.

Ankit, inspired by Riya's experience, starts thinking about his own social media habits. He realizes he often shares a lot of personal information, like his location, school, and even his daily routines, without considering who might be watching.

In their next computer class, the teacher, Mr. Raj, gives a lesson on the risks of oversharing. He explains how cybercriminals can use seemingly harmless information to commit identity theft, stalking, or other malicious activities. Ankit is shocked to learn how easy it is for someone to misuse his information.

Their school organizes a workshop on cyberbullying, a common issue on social media platforms. The guest speaker, a psychologist named Dr. Mehta, shares stories of teenagers who have been victims of online bullying. Riya and Ankit are moved by the stories and realize the importance of standing up against such behavior.

Dr. Mehta emphasizes that cyberbullying can have severe emotional impacts and that it's crucial to report any incidents to trusted adults. She provides tips on how to block and report bullies on different social media platforms.

Mr. Raj continues to educate the class about digital footprints. He explains that everything they post online leaves a trace that can be difficult to erase. Colleges, employers, and even strangers can access this information, which can impact their future opportunities.

Riya and Ankit decide to go through their old posts and remove anything that might be inappropriate or too revealing. They also start thinking twice before posting anything new, considering the long-term implications of their digital actions.

Positive Use of Social Media

Despite the risks, Riya and Ankit learn that social media can also be a positive force when used responsibly. They start following accounts that promote mental health, educational content, and inspiring stories. They participate in online communities that share their interests, like photography for Riya and technology for Ankit.

They also decide to use their platforms to spread awareness about social media safety. Riya starts a blog where she shares tips on protecting personal information, while Ankit makes videos about the importance of strong passwords and recognizing phishing attempts.

Riya and Ankit's journey through the complexities of social media safety teaches them valuable lessons about privacy, responsible sharing, and the potential risks of the digital world. By taking proactive steps to protect themselves and educating others, they turn their social media presence into a force for good.

Their story highlights the importance of awareness and education in navigating social media safely. As we delve deeper into this chapter, we will explore practical strategies for maintaining privacy, recognizing and responding to cyberbullying, and using social media positively and responsibly.

Understanding these aspects is crucial for enjoying the benefits of social media while minimizing its risks, ensuring a safe and enriching digital experience for all.

CHAPTER XXII

Navigating Social Media Platforms Safely

Social media platforms offer numerous benefits, including staying connected with friends and family, sharing experiences, and discovering new content. However, they also pose risks to privacy, security, and mental well-being. Here are some steps to help you navigate social media platforms safely.

Set Strong Privacy Settings - Regularly review and adjust your privacy settings on social media platforms to control who can see your posts, personal information, and activity. Limit your profile visibility to friends only, and avoid making sensitive information public.

Be Mindful of What You Share - Think twice before sharing personal information, such as your address, phone number, or travel plans. Once shared, this information can be difficult to control. Remember that potential employers, schools, or other authorities may view your social media profiles. Keep your content appropriate and professional.

Recognize and Avoid Phishing Scams - Be cautious of messages from unknown contacts that ask for personal information or direct you to click on links. Before clicking on links or downloading attachments, verify the source of the message or email.

Use Strong and Unique Passwords - Use a combination of letters, numbers, and special characters to create strong passwords for your social media accounts. Use unique passwords for each social media platform to prevent a breach on one site from compromising others.

Enable Two-Factor Authentication (2FA) - Enable 2FA on your social media accounts, requiring a second form of verification, such as a code sent to your phone, in addition to your password. This adds an extra layer of security.

Be Cautious with Third-Party Apps - Be selective about which third-party apps you grant access to your social media accounts. Review and remove permissions for apps you no longer use. Ensure that third-party apps do not have access to more information than necessary.

Monitor Your Account Activity - Review your account activity regularly to ensure there are no unauthorized logins or posts. Enable notifications for account logins and suspicious activity to stay informed of any unusual activity.

Educate Yourself About Platform Features - Familiarize yourself with the privacy features and settings offered by each social media platform. Learn how to block and report users who harass or threaten you online.

Be Aware of Location Sharing - Disable location services for social media apps to prevent sharing your real-time location. Avoid geotagging your posts with your exact location, especially if it's your home, school, or workplace.

Manage Friend and Follower Lists - Only accept friend

and follower requests from people you know and trust. Periodically review your friends and followers and remove any that you no longer want to share information with.

Protect Your Mental Well-being - Set limits on how much time you spend on social media to avoid negative impacts on your mental health. Curate your feed to include accounts that promote positivity and well-being. Don't hesitate to take breaks from social media to recharge and refocus.

Stay Informed About Privacy Policies - Understand how social media platforms collect, use, and share your data by reading their privacy policies. Keep informed about any changes to privacy policies and settings to ensure you are always aware of how your data is being handled.

Navigating social media platforms safely requires a proactive approach to privacy and security. By implementing these steps, you can protect your personal information, maintain a positive online presence, and ensure your social media experience is safe and enjoyable. Regularly updating your knowledge and settings is key to staying secure in the ever-evolving digital landscape.

CHAPTER XXIII

Recognizing and Handling Cyberbullying

Cyberbullying is a serious issue that can have significant emotional, psychological, and social impacts. Recognizing the signs of cyberbullying and knowing how to handle it are crucial steps in protecting oneself and others. Here's a guide to help you identify and respond to cyberbullying effectively.

Recognizing Cyberbullying - Cyberbullying can manifest in various forms, such as unwanted messages, public shaming, impersonation, exclusion, threats and intimidation, and cyberstalking. Unwanted messages include persistent negative comments and continuous harassment even after being asked to stop. Public shaming involves publicly sharing humiliating or embarrassing content about someone or spreading false information to damage their reputation. Impersonation includes creating fake profiles to impersonate and harm the victim or using someone else's identity to post harmful content or send messages.

Exclusion entails intentionally excluding someone from online groups, chats, or activities and ignoring someone's messages or interactions as a form of silent treatment. Threats and intimidation cover receiving direct threats of physical harm or blackmail, where private information or images are threatened to be shared unless demands are met. Cyberstalking involves persistent monitoring and tracking of online activity and repeated unwanted attempts to contact or follow someone online.

Handling Cyberbullying - Handling cyberbullying involves several strategies. First, do not engage with the bully. Avoid retaliation and stay calm to prevent the situation from escalating. Save evidence by documenting incidents with screenshots and saving messages, emails, or any other evidence of cyberbullying, noting dates, times, and descriptions of the incidents. Report and block the bully by using the reporting tools provided by social media platforms and blocking the person to prevent further contact and harassment.

Inform trusted adults about the incident, seeking support from parents, teachers, or a trusted adult. If needed, consider professional help from counselors or mental health professionals. Use privacy settings on social media platforms to enhance privacy, limiting who can see your posts and contact you. Regularly review and update your friends or followers list to ensure only trusted people have access.

Know your rights regarding legal protections against cyberbullying in your country, and contact authorities if the cyberbullying involves serious threats or criminal activities. Support others by being an ally to friends or peers experiencing cyberbullying, offering a listening ear, and reporting the incidents. Promote awareness by educating others about the signs of cyberbullying and encouraging them to stand against it.

Take care of yourself by engaging in activities that boost your mental well-being and self-esteem. Consider a digital detox by taking breaks from social media to reduce stress and negative impacts.

Recognizing and handling cyberbullying involves a proactive and informed approach. By understanding the signs of cyberbullying and implementing strategies to address it, you can protect yourself and others from its harmful effects. Remember, seeking help and support is crucial, and no one should have to face cyberbullying alone.

CHAPTER XXIV

Managing Digital Footprints

A digital footprint is the trail of data you leave behind when you use the internet, including your social media activity, websites you visit, emails you send, and any other information you share online. Managing your digital footprint is essential for protecting your privacy, maintaining a positive online reputation, and safeguarding your personal information. Here are steps to effectively manage your digital footprint.

Understanding Digital Footprints - A digital footprint can be either active or passive. An active digital footprint includes data you intentionally share online, such as social media posts, blog comments, and uploaded photos. Examples of this type of data include status updates, tweets, blog posts, and online reviews. On the other hand, a passive digital footprint is the data collected about you without your explicit knowledge, such as browsing history, location data, and cookies. Examples of passive data include websites tracking your visits, online ads based on your search history, and location data from mobile devices.

Steps to Manage Your Digital Footprint - Regularly reviewing your online presence is crucial. Search your name on search engines to see what information is publicly available about you and check your social media profiles to ensure your posts and photos are appropriate and reflect positively on you. Adjust privacy settings on your social media profiles to private so that only approved friends and followers can see your content. Review and limit the permissions of apps on your devices to access your personal data.

Be mindful of what you share online. Think before posting and consider the long-term impact of anything you post. Once shared, content can be difficult to remove completely. Avoid sharing sensitive personal information such as your address, phone number, and financial details. Clean up old accounts by identifying and deleting any old or unused online accounts that may still hold personal information. Close unnecessary subscriptions to reduce the amount of personal data shared.

Manage cookies and tracking by regularly clearing cookies from your browser to remove tracking data and installing extensions that block trackers and ads to reduce passive data collection. Monitor and protect your data by setting up tools like Google Alerts to monitor mentions of your name or personal information online. Sign up for notifications from services like Have I Been Pwned to be informed if your data is compromised in a breach.

Use strong security measures by creating complex, unique passwords for each of your online accounts and enabling two-factor authentication (2FA) for an extra layer of security. Be cautious with third-party apps by only authorizing trusted apps to access your data and reviewing and revoking permissions for apps you no longer use. Read privacy policies to understand how third-party apps use and protect your data before granting access.

Regularly update your software by ensuring your operating systems, browsers, and apps are updated with the latest security patches and installing and regularly updating antivirus software to protect against malware and other threats. Educate yourself about the latest best practices for digital privacy and security, and learn how different online platforms collect and use your data.

Managing your digital footprint is an ongoing process that requires vigilance and proactive measures. By regularly reviewing your online presence, adjusting privacy settings, and being mindful of what you share, you can maintain a positive digital footprint and protect your personal information. Taking these steps will help ensure your online activities remain safe, private, and reflective of your desired online reputation.

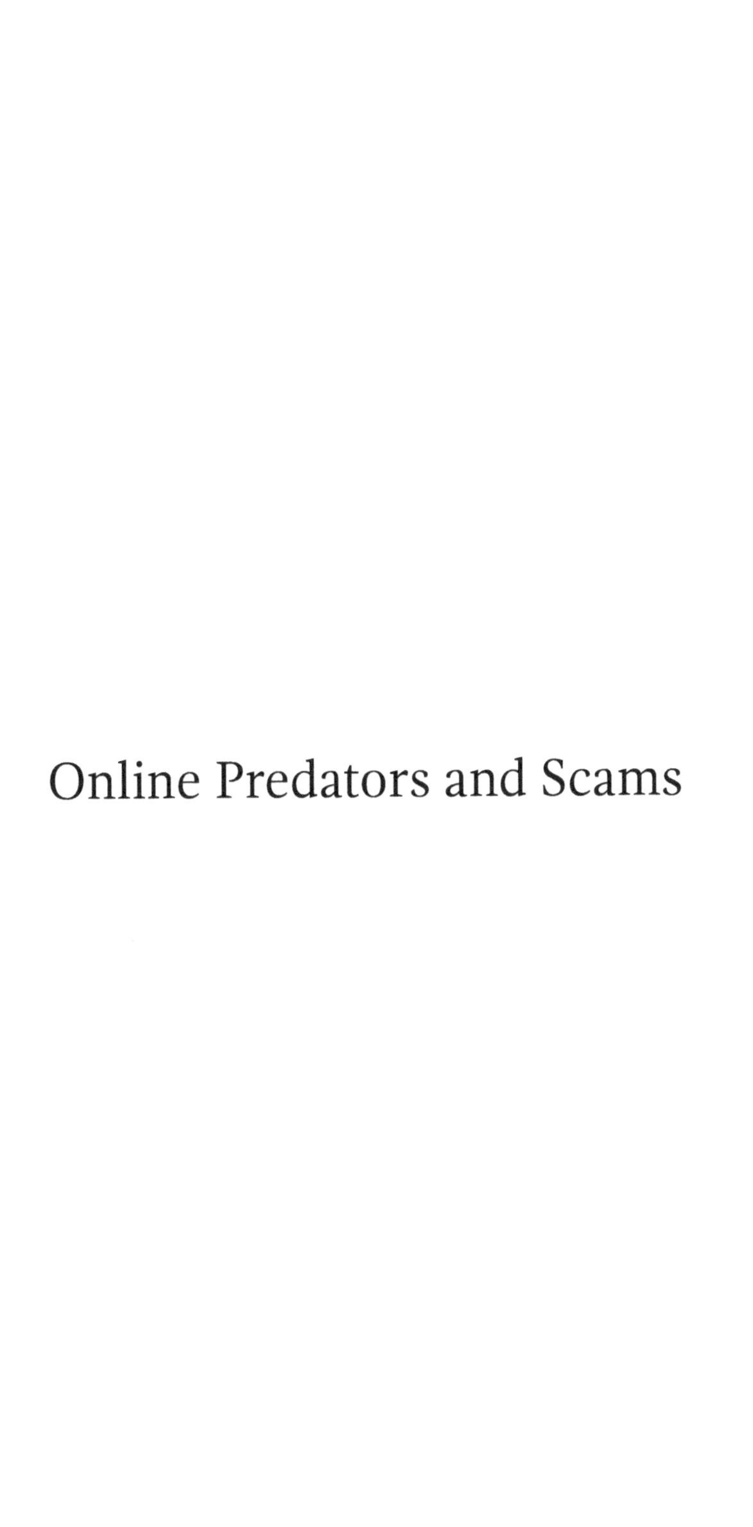

Online Predators and Scams

CHAPTER XXV

The Cautionary Tale of Arjun and Priya

Arjun and Priya, two high school students from Mumbai, are active users of social media and online gaming platforms. They enjoy connecting with friends, sharing photos, and playing multiplayer games. However, their encounter with online predators and scams is about to open their eyes to the darker side of the digital world.

Arjun loves playing online multiplayer games. One evening, while playing his favorite game, he receives a friend request from a user named "CoolGamer123." The user seems friendly, and they quickly bond over their shared interest in the game. "CoolGamer123" often helps Arjun with strategies and sends him virtual gifts in the game.

Over time, Arjun starts sharing more about his personal life with "CoolGamer123," including his school, hobbies, and even his phone number. What Arjun doesn't realize is that not everyone online is who they claim to be.

Priya, on the other hand, is excited when she receives a message on Instagram from a user claiming to be a representative of a popular fashion brand. The message states that she has won a giveaway and can claim a free gift by clicking on a link and filling out a form. The form asks for her name, address, phone number, and even her bank account details to cover shipping costs.

Thrilled by the prospect of winning, Priya fills out the form without thinking twice. She eagerly waits for her gift, but days pass, and she receives nothing. Instead, she notices unauthorized transactions on her bank account.

One day, Arjun's parents notice that he has been unusually quiet and withdrawn. When they ask him what's wrong, he reveals that "CoolGamer123" has started making uncomfortable demands, asking for personal photos and threatening to share their conversations if Arjun doesn't comply. Frightened and unsure what to do, Arjun finally confides in his parents.

Priya, too, feels a growing sense of dread as she realizes she has been scammed. She tells her older brother, who immediately helps her contact the bank to freeze her account and report the fraud.

Arjun's parents take him to the school counselor, Ms. Rao, who has experience dealing with online safety issues. Ms. Rao praises Arjun for coming forward and explains the importance of not sharing personal information with strangers online. She helps him report the incident to the game's support team and advises him to block and remove "CoolGamer123" from his contacts.

Priya's brother, meanwhile, reports the scam to Instagram and helps Priya secure her account. They also file a complaint with the local cybercrime cell. Ms. Rao invites Priya and Arjun to share their experiences in a special assembly on internet safety, hoping to educate their peers about the dangers of online predators and scams.

During the assembly, Priya and Arjun bravely recount their stories. Priya talks about the fake giveaway scam and warns her classmates about the dangers of clicking on suspicious links and sharing personal information online. She emphasizes the importance of verifying the authenticity of messages and offers before acting on them.

Arjun shares his experience with "CoolGamer123" and explains how easy it was to trust someone who seemed friendly and helpful. He talks about the warning signs he missed and the emotional toll the experience took on him. He advises his peers to be cautious about sharing personal information online and to always consult a trusted adult if something feels wrong.

Lessons Learned

The assembly has a profound impact on the students. Many of them start reviewing their online behaviors, tightening privacy settings, and being more skeptical of unsolicited messages and friend requests.

Ms. Rao provides additional resources on recognizing and avoiding online scams, identifying potential predators, and knowing how to report suspicious activities. She encourages open communication between students, parents, and teachers to ensure a safer online environment.

Arjun and Priya's experiences underscore the importance of vigilance and education in navigating the digital world. By sharing their stories, they help their peers understand the potential risks and empower them to protect themselves from online predators and scams.

Their story highlights the need for awareness and proactive measures to ensure online safety. As we explore this chapter further, we will delve into strategies for identifying and avoiding online predators and scams, understanding the tactics used by scammers, and knowing the appropriate steps to take when faced with suspicious activities.

By learning from these experiences, we can create a safer digital environment for everyone, especially for young and impressionable minds navigating the vast online landscape.

CHAPTER XXVI

Identifying Online Threats

The internet offers numerous benefits, but it also presents various threats that can compromise personal information, security, and well-being. Identifying online threats is crucial to protecting yourself and your digital assets. Here are some common online threats and how to recognize them.

Common Online Threats - Phishing involves fraudulent attempts to obtain sensitive information such as usernames, passwords, and credit card details by disguising as a trustworthy entity in electronic communication. Signs of phishing include emails or messages that urge you to click on a link or open an attachment, requests for personal information or financial details, emails with poor grammar and spelling errors, and suspicious email addresses or URLs that mimic legitimate ones (e.g., "faceb00k.com" instead of "facebook.com").

Malware is malicious software designed to harm, exploit, or otherwise compromise a computer or network. Types of malware include viruses, which attach themselves to legitimate programs and replicate; trojans, which disguise as legitimate software but perform malicious actions; ransomware, which encrypts files and demands payment for decryption; and spyware, which secretly monitors user activity and collects information. Signs of malware include slow computer performance, frequent crashes or error messages, unusual pop-ups or ads, and new toolbars or icons that you did not install.

Social engineering involves manipulating individuals into divulging confidential information or performing actions that compromise security. Signs of social engineering include unusual requests for help or information from strangers, attempts to create a sense of urgency or fear to elicit a response, and unsolicited messages from supposed authority figures or acquaintances asking for sensitive information.

Identity theft occurs when someone uses another person's personal information without permission to commit fraud or other crimes. Signs of identity theft include unexplained withdrawals from your bank account, bills or collection notices for accounts you did not open, notifications of data breaches involving your personal information, and unauthorized changes to your account information.

Online scams involve deceptive schemes to trick individuals into giving away money, personal information, or both. Types of online scams include romance scams, where fraudsters pose as romantic interests to gain trust and request money; lottery scams, where victims are told they've won a lottery or prize and need to pay a fee to claim it; and investment scams, which offer false investment opportunities promising high returns. Signs of online scams include requests for money from strangers or online acquaintances, promises of large sums of money for little to no effort, and pressure to act quickly to secure a supposed deal or opportunity.

Cyberbullying involves using digital platforms to harass, threaten, or embarrass individuals. Signs of cyberbullying include repeated negative or threatening messages, public shaming or spreading of false information, impersonation or creation of fake profiles to harass someone, and exclusion from online groups or activities.

Man-in-the-Middle (MitM) attacks occur when an attacker intercepts communication between two parties to steal or manipulate data. Signs of MitM attacks include unexpected changes in your internet connection or website certificates, frequent disconnections or interruptions in your connection, and receiving warnings about insecure connections or certificates.

How to Protect Yourself - Using strong passwords is essential. Create complex passwords with a mix of letters, numbers, and special characters. Avoid using the same password across multiple sites. Use a password manager to securely store and manage your passwords.

Enable two-factor authentication (2FA) for an extra layer of security by requiring a second form of verification, such as a code sent to your phone. Use authenticator apps like Google Authenticator or Authy.

Be skeptical of unsolicited communications. Verify the authenticity of emails, messages, or phone calls requesting personal information or urging you to take immediate action. Use email filters and anti-phishing tools to block suspicious communications.

Keep your software updated. Regularly update your operating system, browser, and applications to protect against known vulnerabilities. Enable automatic updates where possible.

Install security software. Use antivirus and anti-malware software to detect and remove malicious programs. Trusted security software options include Norton, McAfee, and Bitdefender.

Educate yourself and stay informed about the latest online threats and security practices. Participate in cybersecurity awareness programs and follow reputable cybersecurity websites and blogs.

Use secure connections. Avoid using public Wi-Fi for sensitive transactions and use a VPN to encrypt your internet connection. Trusted VPN services include ExpressVPN, NordVPN, and CyberGhost.

Monitor your accounts regularly. Check your bank and credit card statements for unauthorized transactions and set up alerts for suspicious activity. Use financial monitoring services and credit reporting agencies.

Recognizing and addressing online threats is essential for maintaining your digital security and privacy. By staying informed and implementing these protective measures, you can significantly reduce the risk of falling victim to online threats and ensure a safer online experience.

CHAPTER XXVII

Safe Practices for Online Interactions

Online interactions are a significant part of modern life, offering convenience and connectivity. However, they also come with risks. Practicing safe online behavior is crucial to protecting your personal information, maintaining your privacy, and ensuring a positive digital experience. Here are essential practices to follow for safe online interactions.

Protect Personal Information - To safeguard your personal information, limit the sharing of sensitive details such as your home address, phone number, social security number, and financial information. Utilize privacy settings on social media platforms to control who can view your posts and personal information. Additionally, be cautious with the photos you post, avoiding those that reveal personal details about your home, school, or workplace.

Verify Identities - Always question requests for personal information, especially unsolicited messages, even if they seem to come from trusted sources. Confirm the identity of individuals you interact with online, particularly if they ask for personal information or money.

Be Aware of Phishing Scams - Recognize suspicious emails by being cautious of those from unknown senders containing links or attachments. Look for signs of phishing, such as poor grammar and urgent requests. Avoid clicking on unverified links by hovering over them to check the URL before clicking and staying away from links from unknown or suspicious sources.

Use Strong, Unique Passwords - Create complex passwords using a combination of letters, numbers, and special characters, and avoid easily guessable passwords like "password123". Use unique passwords for each online account to prevent a breach on one site from compromising others, and update your passwords periodically to enhance security.

Enable Two-Factor Authentication (2FA) - Add an extra layer of security by enabling 2FA on your accounts, requiring a second form of verification such as a code sent to your phone in addition to your password. Use authenticator apps like Google Authenticator or Authy instead of SMS for better security.

Be Mindful of Public Wi-Fi - Avoid conducting sensitive transactions, such as accessing bank accounts or making purchases, over public Wi-Fi networks. Use a Virtual Private Network (VPN) to encrypt your internet connection and protect your data when using public Wi-Fi.

Secure Your Devices - Use antivirus and anti-malware software to protect your devices from threats, and keep all software, including operating systems, browsers, and apps, regularly updated to guard against security vulnerabilities. Additionally, enable device encryption to protect your data in case your devices are lost or stolen.

Practice Safe Social Media Usage - Regularly review your friends and followers to ensure only trusted individuals have access to your personal information. Be selective with friend requests, accepting only from people you know and trust. Think carefully before posting, considering the long-term impact and potential audience of your posts, as once something is online, it can be difficult to remove completely.

Be Cautious with Downloads and Links - Download software and apps only from official and trusted websites or app stores. Avoid clicking on links in unsolicited messages or emails, and always verify the source before opening any link.

Report Suspicious Activity - Use the reporting tools provided by social media platforms to report cyberbullying, harassment, or other suspicious activities. If you encounter serious threats, fraud, or criminal activity, report it to the appropriate authorities or law enforcement.

Practicing safe online interactions involves being vigilant, using security tools, and making informed decisions about sharing personal information. By following these safe practices, you can protect yourself from online threats and enjoy a more secure and positive digital experience. Regularly updating your knowledge and staying aware of new threats will further enhance your online safety.

CHAPTER XXVIII

Reporting and Responding to Suspicious Activities

Identifying and responding to suspicious activities online is essential to protect yourself and others from potential threats such as cyberbullying, fraud, and other malicious actions. Here's a guide on how to effectively report and respond to suspicious activities.

Recognizing Suspicious Activities - Unusual account activity can be a significant indicator of suspicious behavior. Look out for unauthorized logins or attempts to access your accounts, unexpected changes to account settings or personal information, and security alerts about password changes or login attempts.

Phishing attempts are another common threat. Be wary of emails or messages asking for personal information or containing suspicious links, especially if they come from unknown senders with urgent or alarming content. Communications that mimic legitimate organizations but have subtle differences in email addresses or URLs should also raise red flags.

Fraud and scams often involve requests for money or personal information from unknown contacts. Offers that seem too good to be true, such as winning a lottery you didn't enter, and messages urging immediate action to avoid consequences, like account suspension, are typical signs of scams.

Cyberbullying and harassment can manifest as threatening or abusive messages, public shaming, or embarrassing content posted about you. Being repeatedly targeted by the same individual or group is a clear sign of cyberbullying.

Malware and viruses can cause sudden slowdowns in your device's performance, frequent crashes, unexpected pop-ups, and unknown programs or files appearing on your device.

Steps to Report Suspicious Activities - When encountering suspicious activities, start by documenting the evidence. Capture screenshots of suspicious messages, emails, or account activity, save copies of these communications, and record details such as dates, times, and other relevant information.

Next, report the issue to the platform where it occurred. Use built-in reporting tools available on most social media platforms, email providers, and online services. If these tools are not available, contact the customer support team of the platform or service.

Notify relevant authorities if the incident is serious. Report cases of fraud, threats, or cyberbullying to your local cybercrime unit or law enforcement agency. For financial fraud or identity theft, immediately contact your bank or credit card company.

If the suspicious activity occurs at work or school, report it to your IT or security department. Follow your organization's protocols for reporting and responding to security incidents.

Responding to Suspicious Activities - To respond to suspicious activities, start by securing your accounts.

Change the passwords of any compromised accounts using strong, unique passwords, and enable two-factor authentication (2FA) for added security.

Scan your devices for malware using reputable antivirus software, and remove any threats. Ensure your operating system and all applications are updated with the latest security patches.

Inform your contacts about the situation. Notify friends, family, or colleagues if your accounts have been compromised so they can be cautious of any suspicious messages they might receive from you. If you received a phishing attempt, alert others to prevent them from falling victim.

Monitor your accounts regularly. Check your bank and credit card statements for unauthorized transactions, and set up account alerts to receive notifications of any unusual activity.

If the situation is complex or severe, seek professional help. Consult cybersecurity experts for technical assistance and talk to a counselor or mental health professional if you are experiencing stress or anxiety due to cyberbullying or harassment.

Reporting and responding to suspicious activities promptly and effectively is crucial to protecting your personal information, security, and well-being. By following these steps, you can mitigate the impact of online threats and contribute to a safer digital environment for yourself and others. Stay vigilant and proactive in monitoring and securing your online presence.

Cybersecurity Essentials

CHAPTER XXIX

The Cybersecurity Awakening of Ravi and Meera

Ravi and Meera, high school students from Bangalore, are tech-savvy teens who enjoy the digital world. Ravi is passionate about coding and dreams of becoming a software engineer, while Meera loves photography and frequently shares her work online. Their journey into understanding cybersecurity essentials begins with a series of incidents that make them realize the importance of protecting their digital lives.

One morning, Ravi receives an email that appears to be from his favorite online gaming platform, offering him exclusive in-game items for free. Excited, he clicks on the link provided in the email and logs in using his account credentials. However, within hours, he notices strange activities on his account—items are missing, and his in-game currency has been depleted.

Ravi's heart sinks as he realizes he has been a victim of a phishing scam. He quickly changes his password and contacts the platform's support team to report the incident. This experience leaves him shaken and more cautious about online activities.

Meanwhile, Meera gets a friend request on social media from someone claiming to be a fellow photographer interested in collaborating. Flattered, she accepts the request and starts chatting with the person. They soon ask her to download a file containing "collaboration ideas." Without thinking, Meera downloads and opens the file, which turns out to be malware that corrupts her computer and threatens to delete her precious photos.

Panicked, Meera tells her parents, who take her to a local computer repair shop. The technician explains that the file contained a virus and helps clean her computer, but some data is lost. This incident makes Meera realize the dangers of downloading files from untrusted sources.

A Cybersecurity Workshop

Their school, noticing the increase in cyber incidents among students, organizes a cybersecurity workshop led by an expert, Mr. Sharma. Ravi and Meera, along with their classmates, attend the workshop eagerly.

Mr. Sharma starts by explaining the basics of cybersecurity, emphasizing the importance of strong passwords, recognizing phishing attempts, and avoiding suspicious downloads. He shares practical tips, such as using a password manager to create and store unique passwords and enabling two-factor authentication on all accounts.

Mr. Sharma demonstrates how easy it is for hackers to crack weak passwords using automated tools. He shows the class how to create strong, complex passwords that include a mix of letters, numbers, and special characters. He also stresses the importance of not reusing passwords across different sites.

Inspired by this, Ravi changes all his passwords to stronger ones and starts using a password manager. He also helps his friends understand the importance of doing the same.

Mr. Sharma then moves on to phishing, explaining how scammers use deceptive emails, messages, or websites to trick people into revealing personal information. He provides examples of common phishing tactics and red flags to watch out for, such as urgent language, suspicious links, and unexpected attachments.

Meera realizes how easily she fell for the fake collaboration request and learns to scrutinize messages more carefully. She resolves to verify the identity of anyone asking for personal information or downloads in the future.

The workshop also covers two-factor authentication (2FA), which adds an extra layer of security by requiring a second form of verification in addition to a password. Mr. Sharma shows the students how to enable 2FA on popular platforms and explains how it can protect them even if their passwords are compromised.

Both Ravi and Meera activate 2FA on their accounts, feeling more secure knowing that their data has an additional layer of protection.

Mr. Sharma emphasizes the importance of safe browsing practices, such as avoiding suspicious websites and being cautious about the information shared online. He also explains the significance of keeping software and devices updated, as updates often include security patches that protect against vulnerabilities.

Ravi and Meera make it a habit to regularly update their devices and software, ensuring they have the latest security protections.

Empowered by the workshop, Ravi and Meera decide to spread awareness about cybersecurity among their peers. They create a presentation highlighting key points from the workshop and share it during their computer science class. They also start a blog where they post tips on staying safe online, share their own experiences, and encourage others to adopt good cybersecurity practices.

Ravi and Meera's journey into the world of cybersecurity teaches them valuable lessons about protecting their digital identities. Their experiences highlight the importance of strong passwords, recognizing phishing attempts, enabling two-factor authentication, and practicing safe browsing.

As we delve into this chapter, we will explore these cybersecurity essentials in greater detail, providing practical steps and strategies to help you safeguard your digital life. By understanding and implementing these practices, you can navigate the online world with confidence and security, just like Ravi and Meera.

CHAPTER XXX

Understanding Common Cyber Threats

Cyber threats are malicious activities that target computers, networks, and online systems, aiming to steal, damage, or disrupt data and services. Understanding these threats is essential for protecting yourself and your digital assets. Here are some of the most common cyber threats and how to recognize them.

Common Cyber Threats - Phishing involves fraudulent attempts to obtain sensitive information by disguising as a trustworthy entity in electronic communication. There are various types of phishing, including email phishing, where fake emails appear to be from legitimate sources requesting personal information or urging you to click on malicious links; spear phishing, which targets specific individuals or organizations using personalized information; and smishing and vishing, which are phishing attacks via SMS and voice calls, respectively. Signs of phishing include urgent or threatening language, requests for personal or financial information, and suspicious links or attachments.

Malware is malicious software designed to harm, exploit, or otherwise compromise a computer system or network. Types of malware include viruses, which attach themselves to legitimate files and spread to other files and systems; trojans, which disguise themselves as legitimate applications; ransomware, which encrypts a victim's files and demands payment for the decryption key; spyware, which secretly monitors user activity and collects information; and adware, which displays unwanted ads and may track user behavior. Signs of malware include slow computer performance, frequent crashes or error messages, unusual pop-ups or ads, and new toolbars or icons that you did not install.

Ransomware specifically encrypts a victim's files, making them inaccessible, and demands a ransom payment for the decryption key. Signs of ransomware include the inability to access files, a ransom note displayed on your screen, and instructions for paying the ransom to regain access to your files.

Social engineering involves manipulating individuals into divulging confidential information or performing actions that compromise security. Types of social engineering include pretexting, where a fabricated scenario is created to steal personal information; baiting, which offers something enticing to lure victims into a trap; and quid pro quo, which promises a service or benefit in exchange for information. Signs of social engineering include unusual requests for help or information from strangers, attempts to create a sense of urgency or fear, and unsolicited messages from supposed authority figures or acquaintances asking for sensitive information.

Denial of Service (DoS) and Distributed Denial of Service (DDoS) attacks aim to overwhelm a system, server, or network with traffic, rendering it unusable. Signs of these attacks include slow network performance, the inability to access a website or service, and large amounts of spam emails.

Man-in-the-Middle (MitM) attacks occur when an attacker intercepts communication between two parties to steal or manipulate data. Types of MitM attacks include eavesdropping, where communications are intercepted and monitored, and session hijacking, where a user session is taken over to gain unauthorized access. Signs of MitM attacks include unexpected changes in your internet connection or website certificates, frequent disconnections or interruptions in your connection, and receiving warnings about insecure connections or certificates.

SQL injection involves inserting malicious SQL code into a query to manipulate or access a database. Signs of SQL injection include unusual behavior from a web application, unauthorized access to data, and error messages related to database queries.

Password attacks involve attempting to obtain or decrypt a user's password. Types of password attacks include brute force attacks, where all possible password combinations are tried until the correct one is found; dictionary attacks, which use a list of common passwords to attempt access; and credential stuffing, which uses leaked username and password pairs to gain unauthorized access. Signs of password attacks include account lockouts, unauthorized account access, and multiple failed login attempts.

How to Protect Yourself - Using strong passwords is crucial. Create complex passwords with a mix of letters, numbers, and special characters, and avoid reusing passwords across multiple sites. Enable two-factor authentication (2FA) to add an extra layer of security, requiring a second form of verification in addition to your password.

Keeping your software updated is essential. Regularly update your operating system, browsers, and applications with the latest security patches. Be wary of suspicious emails and links by verifying the sources and hovering over links to check the URL before clicking. Avoid clicking on links or downloading attachments from unknown or suspicious sources.

Use security software, such as antivirus and anti-malware programs, and regularly update and run scans. Enable a firewall to block unauthorized access to your network. Educate yourself and stay informed about the latest cyber threats and best practices for protecting yourself. Participate in security awareness programs offered by employers or educational institutions.

Understanding common cyber threats is the first step toward protecting yourself and your digital assets. By staying informed and implementing strong security practices, you can reduce the risk of falling victim to cyber-attacks and ensure a safer online experience. Regularly review and update your security measures to stay ahead of evolving threats.

CHAPTER XXXI

Importance of Strong Passwords

Passwords are the first line of defense in protecting your online accounts and personal information. Using strong passwords is essential to safeguarding your digital life from unauthorized access, cyber-attacks, and data breaches. Understanding the importance of strong passwords and learning how to create and manage them effectively is crucial in today's digital age.

Why Strong Passwords Are Important - Strong passwords provide protection against unauthorized access, preventing account hijacking by making it difficult for unauthorized users to guess or crack your passwords. They also safeguard sensitive information, ensuring that your personal and financial data remain secure from cybercriminals. In terms of defense against cyber-attacks, strong passwords significantly increase the time and effort required to crack them, making brute force and dictionary attacks much less effective. This is because strong passwords use a mix of characters and are resistant to common words or patterns.

Strong passwords also play a vital role in preventing identity theft. By securing your personal information, they help prevent cybercriminals from using your data for fraudulent activities. Additionally, protecting your financial accounts with strong passwords ensures that your money and financial identity are safe from compromise. Compliance with security standards is another critical aspect, as many organizations require employees to use strong passwords to protect sensitive corporate data and meet regulatory requirements for data protection and cybersecurity.

Moreover, having strong passwords provides peace of mind. Knowing that your accounts are secured reduces anxiety about potential cyber threats and lowers the overall risk of data breaches and cyber incidents.

Characteristics of Strong Passwords - Strong passwords should be lengthy, with a minimum of 12 characters, as longer passwords are exponentially harder to crack. They should also be complex, using a mix of uppercase and lowercase letters, numbers, and special characters while avoiding easily guessable patterns like "123456," "password," or "qwerty." Uniqueness is crucial; each account should have a unique password to prevent a breach on one site from compromising others, and reusing passwords across multiple sites should be avoided. Randomness is another key characteristic; passwords should not include personal information such as names or birthdays and should be created using random combinations that do not follow predictable patterns.

Using a password manager is highly recommended for generating strong passwords and storing them securely. Password managers can create complex and random passwords for you, ensuring that each password is unique and strong without the need for you to remember them all. Regularly updating your passwords is another important practice. Change your passwords periodically to reduce the risk of long-term exposure and immediately update any passwords that you suspect have been compromised.

Enabling two-factor authentication (2FA) adds an extra layer of security by requiring a second form of verification, such as a code sent to your phone, in addition to your password. Authenticator apps like Google Authenticator or Authy are preferred over SMS for better security. Educating yourself and staying informed about password security best practices and common password-related threats is also crucial. By staying updated, you can better protect your accounts and personal information.

Strong passwords are a critical component of your overall cybersecurity strategy. They protect your accounts from unauthorized access, safeguard your personal and financial information, and provide peace of mind. By creating complex, unique, and random passwords, using tools like password managers and two-factor authentication, and regularly updating your passwords, you can significantly enhance your online security. Staying informed about best practices will help ensure your digital life remains secure.

CHAPTER XXXII

Using Two-Factor Authentication

Two-Factor Authentication (2FA) is an additional layer of security designed to ensure that individuals trying to gain access to an online account are who they claim to be. Initially, a user will enter their username and password. Instead of gaining immediate access, they will be required to provide another piece of information. This second factor could come from one of the following categories: something you know, like a second password, PIN, or answer to a secret question; something you have, such as a smartphone, hardware token, or email account; or something you are, involving biometrics like fingerprints, retina scans, or voice recognition.

Benefits of Two-Factor Authentication - The primary benefit of 2FA is enhanced security. It significantly reduces the risk of unauthorized access because, even if a password is compromised, the second factor must also be breached. This added layer of protection is particularly effective against phishing attacks, where a hacker might have obtained your password. Additionally, 2FA helps in meeting regulatory requirements, as many industries and regulatory bodies mandate the use of 2FA to comply with data protection and cybersecurity standards. Furthermore, 2FA provides peace of mind, improving confidence in account security and reducing anxiety about potential breaches.

Setting up 2FA typically involves enabling it in the security settings of your online accounts. Look for options like "Security," "Login settings," or "Account protection."

During setup, you will choose a second factor, which could be an authenticator app, SMS, email, or hardware token. Authenticator apps, such as Google Authenticator, Authy, or Microsoft Authenticator, generate time-based one-time passcodes (TOTP). Alternatively, codes can be sent via SMS or email, or you can use hardware tokens like YubiKey or RSA SecurID. Biometric methods include fingerprint scans and facial recognition.

The authentication process begins with entering your username and password as usual. Then, you provide the second factor for authentication, which could be a code from your authenticator app, a code sent via SMS, or a biometric scan. Upon successful verification of both factors, access to the account is granted.

Implementing Two-Factor Authentication

To enable 2FA on major platforms, follow these steps:

For Google, go to your Google Account settings, select "Security," then "2-Step Verification" to set up 2FA. For Facebook, navigate to "Settings & Privacy," then "Security and Login," and turn on "Two-Factor Authentication." On Twitter, go to "Settings and privacy," select "Security and account access," then "Security," and enable "Two-Factor Authentication." For Amazon, visit "Login & Security" under "Your Account," and enable "Two-Step Verification."

Best practices for using 2FA include using authenticator apps over SMS, as they are generally more secure against SIM-swapping attacks. Keep backup codes safe; most services provide these codes during setup for emergency access. Regularly update your recovery information to ensure that your recovery phone number and email address are current.

If you lose access to your second factor, use the backup codes provided during the setup of 2FA. If necessary, contact the service provider's support team for account recovery options or update your 2FA method using alternative verification options provided by the service.

Two-Factor Authentication significantly enhances the security of your online accounts by requiring a second form of verification in addition to your password. This additional layer of security makes it much more difficult for unauthorized users to gain access, even if they have your password. By enabling 2FA, using strong authentication methods, and following best practices, you can protect your personal information and ensure a safer online experience.

Digital Well-being and
Mental Health

CHAPTER XXXIII

The Story of Ayesha and Raj

Ayesha and Raj are two high school students from Hyderabad. Both are active on social media and spend considerable time online, whether for schoolwork, connecting with friends, or pursuing their hobbies. As they navigate the digital world, they face challenges that impact their mental health and digital well-being.

The Allure of Social Media - Ayesha loves sharing her art on Instagram. Her feed is filled with vibrant paintings and sketches, and she often receives positive feedback from her followers. However, she finds herself constantly checking her phone for new likes and comments. The validation she receives online becomes addictive, and she starts spending hours perfecting her posts, seeking approval from her virtual audience.

Raj, on the other hand, is an avid gamer who enjoys playing multiplayer games. He often stays up late, competing with friends and strangers online. The thrill of the game keeps him hooked, but he begins to notice that his school performance is slipping, and he feels tired and irritable during the day.

The Impact on Mental Health - Ayesha's self-esteem begins to fluctuate with the number of likes and comments she receives. On days when her posts don't perform well, she feels inadequate and questions her artistic abilities. The pressure to maintain a perfect online persona starts to take a toll on her mental health, leading to anxiety and stress.

Raj's late-night gaming sessions affect his sleep schedule, making it difficult for him to concentrate in class. He also experiences moments of frustration and anger when he loses games or faces online harassment from other players. The lack of sleep and constant exposure to competitive gaming environments leave him feeling mentally and emotionally drained.

A Wake-Up Call - One day, during a school assembly, a guest speaker from a local mental health organization talks about the importance of digital well-being. The speaker highlights the signs of digital addiction, the impact of social media on self-esteem, and the effects of excessive screen time on mental health. Ayesha and Raj listen attentively, realizing that they identify with many of the issues discussed.

Motivated by the talk, Ayesha decides to take a break from social media. She starts by limiting her screen time and setting specific hours for checking her accounts. She also begins practicing mindfulness and spends more time on her art without the pressure of posting it online.

Raj, inspired by the speaker, decides to establish a healthier gaming routine. He sets a curfew for his gaming sessions, ensuring he gets enough sleep. He also explores other hobbies, such as reading and playing cricket with friends, to diversify his activities and reduce his screen time.

Finding Balance - Ayesha discovers that taking breaks from social media helps her reconnect with her passion for art. Without the constant need for validation, she feels more creative and satisfied with her work. She also starts a journal to reflect on her feelings and experiences, which helps her manage her anxiety and stress.

Raj finds that getting enough sleep and spending time on offline activities improves his overall well-being. He feels more focused in school and enjoys his gaming sessions more when they are balanced with other interests. He also learns to handle online interactions better, avoiding toxic players and reporting harassment when necessary.

Promoting Digital Well-being - Inspired by their personal growth, Ayesha and Raj decide to promote digital well-being among their peers. They collaborate with their school counselor to organize workshops on managing screen time, recognizing signs of digital addiction, and maintaining mental health in the digital age.

During these workshops, Ayesha shares her journey of finding balance and the importance of disconnecting from social media. Raj talks about his experience with gaming and the benefits of a healthy digital routine. They also provide practical tips and resources, such as apps for tracking screen time and mindfulness exercises.

Ayesha and Raj's story highlights the importance of digital well-being and mental health. Their experiences underscore the need for balance in the digital world, recognizing the signs of digital addiction, and taking proactive steps to maintain mental health.

As we explore this chapter, we will delve deeper into the concepts of digital well-being and mental health, offering strategies and tools to help you achieve a healthier relationship with technology. By understanding and prioritizing your mental health, you can navigate the digital landscape with resilience and well-being, just like Ayesha and Raj.

CHAPTER XXXIV

Impact of Digital Usage on Mental Health

Digital technology has become an integral part of our lives, offering numerous benefits such as connectivity, access to information, and entertainment. However, excessive or inappropriate digital usage can negatively impact mental health, especially among teens. Understanding these impacts is crucial for promoting healthy digital habits.

Positive Impacts of Digital Usage - Digital usage offers several positive impacts, including enhanced connectivity and social support. Social media and messaging apps enable people to stay in touch with friends and family, providing social support and reducing feelings of loneliness. Online communities offer support groups for individuals with similar interests or challenges, fostering a sense of belonging and understanding. Additionally, the Internet provides access to a wealth of educational resources, enhancing learning opportunities. Online platforms offer resources and information on mental health issues, helping individuals understand and manage their conditions. Moreover, digital platforms allow for creative expression through blogs, videos, art, and music, which can be therapeutic and fulfilling. Access to entertainment such as movies, games, and music can provide relaxation and enjoyment, contributing to overall well-being.

Negative Impacts of Digital Usage - Despite these benefits, digital usage can also have negative impacts. Social media often showcases idealized images and lifestyles, leading to unrealistic comparisons and feelings of inadequacy. Constant exposure to curated and filtered content can negatively impact self-esteem and body image. The anonymity of the internet can facilitate cyberbullying and harassment, causing significant emotional distress. Victims of cyberbullying may withdraw from social interactions, leading to increased feelings of loneliness and isolation. Excessive use of digital devices and platforms can lead to addiction, characterized by compulsive usage and difficulty in controlling screen time. Digital addiction can interfere with daily responsibilities, academic performance, and personal relationships. The blue light emitted by screens can disrupt the production of melatonin, a hormone that regulates sleep, leading to poor sleep quality. Excessive digital usage, particularly late at night, can reduce overall sleep duration, impacting mental and physical health. Constant exposure to news and information, particularly negative content, can contribute to anxiety and stress. The pressure to stay constantly connected and updated can lead to anxiety and feelings of inadequacy.

Strategies for Healthy Digital Usage - To mitigate these negative impacts, it is important to set boundaries and limits on digital usage. Set daily limits on screen time to prevent excessive usage and use built-in tools and apps to monitor and control screen time. Take regular breaks from digital devices to rest your eyes and mind. Promote balanced activities by incorporating physical activities and exercise into your daily routine to balance screen time and improve overall well-being. Engage in offline hobbies and activities that provide joy and relaxation. Encourage mindful usage by being purposeful with your digital usage and using technology as a tool rather than a default activity. Periodically take a break from digital devices to reset and recharge. Create a healthy digital environment by following accounts and engaging with content that promotes positivity and well-being. Unfollow or mute accounts that contribute to negative feelings or stress. Foster real-life connections by prioritizing face-to-face interactions with friends and family to build strong, supportive relationships. Participate in social activities and community events to enhance your sense of belonging. Educate yourself about digital literacy by developing critical thinking skills to evaluate online content and recognize misinformation. Learn and practice safe online behavior to protect your mental and emotional well-being.

While digital technology offers numerous benefits, it is essential to manage digital usage to mitigate its negative impacts on mental health. By setting boundaries, promoting balanced activities, and fostering a healthy digital environment, individuals can enjoy the advantages of technology while maintaining their mental well-being. Awareness and education about the potential risks and healthy practices are crucial for cultivating a balanced and positive digital experience.

CHAPTER XXXV

Balancing Screen Time and Real Life

Balancing screen time with real-life activities is crucial for maintaining mental and physical well-being. Excessive screen time can lead to a range of issues, including eye strain, poor sleep, and decreased physical activity. Implementing strategies to manage screen time effectively can enhance your overall quality of life.

Strategies for Balancing Screen Time - Setting clear boundaries is an important first step. Designate screen-free zones in your home, such as the dining room or bedrooms, to encourage screen-free interactions. Create screen time schedules by allocating specific times of the day for screen use and avoiding screens during meals and an hour before bedtime. Use technology wisely by monitoring your screen time with apps and device settings that track and limit your usage. Enable blue light filters on your devices, especially in the evening, to reduce eye strain and improve sleep quality.

Incorporating physical activity into your daily routine is essential. Schedule regular exercise such as walking, running, or playing sports, aiming for at least 30 minutes of moderate exercise daily. Take short breaks from screens to stretch, move around, and rest your eyes, following the 20-20-20 rule: every 20 minutes, look at something 20 feet away for at least 20 seconds.

Prioritizing real-life interactions can also help balance screen time. Make time for in-person conversations and activities with family and friends, and plan social activities that do not involve screens. Engage in community events, clubs, or volunteer work to build real-life connections and contribute to your local community.

Developing hobbies and interests that do not involve screens can be fulfilling. Explore offline activities such as reading, cooking, gardening, or crafting, and set personal goals related to these hobbies. Create a healthy digital environment by following accounts and engaging with content that promotes positivity and well-being, and avoid content that leads to negative feelings or stress. Periodically take a break from digital devices with a digital detox to reset and recharge, planning days or weekends where you disconnect entirely.

Practicing mindfulness and self-care can improve your relationship with screens. Be conscious of your screen time and reflect on how it affects your well-being. Incorporate self-care activities such as meditation, journaling, or spending time in nature into your daily routine. Establish a sleep-friendly routine by maintaining a regular sleep schedule and avoiding screens at least an hour before bedtime to improve sleep quality. Create a relaxing bedtime routine that promotes restful sleep.

Educating yourself and others about the effects of screen time on mental and physical health is crucial. Stay informed about the potential impacts of excessive screen time and share strategies and tips with family and friends to encourage healthy habits within your community.

Implementing Balance in Different Contexts - For students, scheduling regular breaks during study sessions to rest your eyes and move around is essential. Use these breaks for physical activities or mindfulness exercises and use screen time productively for educational purposes while limiting recreational use during study periods. For professionals, maintaining a work-life balance is key. Set boundaries between work and personal time, avoiding work-related tasks outside of designated hours. Create an ergonomic workspace to reduce physical strain during screen use by ensuring proper posture, lighting, and screen placement. For families, planning regular activities that do not involve screens, such as board games, outdoor adventures, or cooking together, can be beneficial. Lead by example and practice healthy screen time habits yourself to encourage similar behavior in your children.

Balancing screen time and real-life activities is essential for maintaining mental and physical health. By setting clear boundaries, incorporating physical activity, prioritizing real-life interactions, and practicing mindfulness, you can create a healthier relationship with digital devices. Implementing these strategies will help you enjoy the benefits of technology while ensuring a fulfilling and balanced life.

CHAPTER XXXVI

Recognizing Signs of Digital Addiction

Digital addiction, also known as internet addiction or technology addiction, refers to excessive and compulsive use of digital devices such as smartphones, computers, and gaming consoles. This behavior can interfere with daily life, responsibilities, and overall well-being. Recognizing the signs of digital addiction is the first step toward addressing the issue and seeking help.

Common Signs of Digital Addiction - Preoccupation with digital devices is a primary sign of digital addiction. This includes constantly checking your phone, social media, or email, even when it's not necessary, and frequently thinking about online activities or anticipating the next online session. Another significant sign is the loss of control, where individuals find it difficult to limit or control their time spent on digital devices and repeatedly fail in attempts to cut back.

Neglect of responsibilities is another common indicator. Those suffering from digital addiction often ignore obligations such as school, work, or household duties due to excessive digital use, leading to decreased productivity in academic or work performance. Withdrawal symptoms, such as irritability, anxiety, mood swings, or depression when offline, are also prevalent among those with digital addiction.

Tolerance and escalation are other critical signs, where individuals need to spend more time on digital devices to achieve the same level of satisfaction and seek more intense online experiences. This addiction can also lead to neglect of physical health, resulting in sleep disturbances, poor hygiene, and diet, along with physical symptoms like eye strain, headaches, or back pain due to prolonged device use.

Digital addiction can significantly impact relationships, leading to social isolation and conflicts with loved ones about the amount of time spent online. People may use digital devices to escape reality, avoiding responsibilities or difficult situations, and preferring digital activities over previously enjoyed hobbies and sports. Risky behaviors, such as engaging in unsafe online practices or neglecting safety precautions, are also common.

Addressing Digital Addiction - Addressing digital addiction begins with self-assessment and awareness. Reflect on your digital usage and its impact on your life, and use apps or device settings to monitor and track your screen time. Setting boundaries and limits is crucial, including creating a daily schedule that limits screen time and designating specific times of the day when digital devices are not allowed, such as during meals or before bedtime.

Seeking support from loved ones or professional help from a mental health professional specializing in digital addiction can provide necessary guidance and encouragement. Developing healthy habits, such as engaging in regular physical exercise and exploring offline hobbies like reading, gardening, or cooking, can also help reduce reliance on digital devices.

Practicing mindfulness in digital usage involves making conscious decisions about when and how to use digital devices and incorporating relaxation techniques such as meditation, deep breathing, or yoga to manage stress. Creating a healthy digital environment by following positive online content and periodically taking breaks from digital devices, known as digital detox, can also contribute to a balanced digital life.

Recognizing the signs of digital addiction is crucial for taking proactive steps to address the issue. By setting boundaries, seeking support, and developing healthy habits, you can achieve a balanced relationship with digital technology and improve your overall well-being. Awareness and mindful usage are key to maintaining a healthy digital life.

Safe Online Gaming

CHAPTER XXXVII

The Adventures of Aryan and Kavya

Aryan and Kavya, two teenagers from Pune, share a common passion for online gaming. Aryan, a high school sophomore, is known for his strategic thinking and loves playing multiplayer battle royale games. Kavya, a year younger, enjoys adventure and puzzle games that challenge her intellect and creativity. Their gaming experiences are filled with excitement, but they soon learn the importance of safe online gaming practices.

The Excitement of Online Gaming - Aryan and Kavya often discuss their gaming achievements during school breaks. Aryan recounts his thrilling victories in intense battles, while Kavya shares her progress in solving intricate puzzles. They both appreciate the skills they develop through gaming, such as problem-solving, teamwork, and quick decision-making.

One weekend, Aryan invites Kavya to join his gaming squad for a marathon session. They plan to play for hours, aiming to reach higher ranks and unlock exclusive rewards. As they immerse themselves in the virtual world, they encounter various challenges and interactions with other players.

Encountering Online Threats - During their gaming marathon, Aryan receives a friend request from a player named "DragonMaster" who promises to share cheats and hacks to help them win more games. Intrigued, Aryan accepts the request and starts chatting with DragonMaster.

The player asks Aryan to download a file, claiming it will enhance his gaming performance. Aryan hesitates, remembering the warnings about malware and scams, but curiosity gets the better of him.

Meanwhile, Kavya faces a different issue. She encounters a player who repeatedly sends her inappropriate messages and makes her uncomfortable. Kavya feels unsure about how to handle the situation, as she doesn't want to ruin her gaming experience by engaging with the player.

Learning Safe Practices - Aryan and Kavya decide to talk to their friend Rishi, who is known for his knowledge of cybersecurity and safe online practices. They meet Rishi after school and share their experiences. Rishi listens carefully and provides valuable advice.

Rishi explains the dangers of downloading cheats and hacks. He tells Aryan that such files often contain malware that can harm his computer and compromise his personal information. Rishi advises Aryan to uninstall any suspicious software and run a security scan on his computer. He also suggests sticking to official game updates and patches to ensure a safe gaming experience.

Rishi then addresses Kavya's concern about inappropriate messages. He explains the importance of reporting and blocking players who engage in harassment. Rishi shows Kavya how to use the reporting features within the game and encourages her to take immediate action to protect herself. He also advises her to avoid sharing personal information with strangers online.

Implementing Safe Gaming Practices - Armed with Rishi's

advice, Aryan and Kavya take steps to ensure their online safety. Aryan removes the suspicious file from his computer and updates his security software. He also shares the importance of avoiding cheats and hacks with his gaming squad, emphasizing that fair play enhances the overall gaming experience.

Kavya reports the player who harassed her and blocks them from further contact. She feels a sense of relief knowing she has taken control of the situation. Kavya also decides to join online communities that promote safe and respectful gaming environments, where players support each other and share positive experiences.

Promoting Safe Gaming - Inspired by their experiences, Aryan and Kavya decide to raise awareness about safe online gaming practices among their peers. They collaborate with their school's computer science teacher to organize a workshop on online safety for gamers. During the workshop, they share their stories and provide practical tips on avoiding scams, handling harassment, and protecting personal information.

Aryan and Kavya also create a blog where they write about their gaming adventures and share advice on safe gaming practices. They include resources such as links to official game support pages, cybersecurity tips, and guides on reporting inappropriate behavior.

Aryan and Kavya's story highlights the importance of safe online gaming practices. Their experiences underscore the need to be vigilant about potential threats, avoid suspicious downloads, and handle harassment appropriately. By implementing these practices, they not only protect themselves but also contribute to creating a safer and more enjoyable gaming community.

As we delve into this chapter, we will explore various aspects of safe online gaming, providing strategies and tools to help you navigate the digital gaming world securely. By understanding and adopting these practices, you can enjoy your gaming adventures with confidence and peace of mind, just like Aryan and Kavya.

CHAPTER XXXVIII

Risks in Online Gaming

Online gaming is a popular form of entertainment that connects players worldwide. While it offers numerous benefits, such as social interaction, cognitive development, and stress relief, it also comes with various risks. Understanding these risks is essential for ensuring a safe and enjoyable gaming experience.

Common Risks in Online Gaming - Cyberbullying and harassment are prevalent in online gaming, where players may be targeted with offensive, threatening, or humiliating messages. Signs of this include receiving abusive messages, being targeted in-game, and experiencing social exclusion from other players. Another risk is exposure to inappropriate content, particularly for younger players who might encounter violence, explicit language, or sexual material within games. This can manifest through in-game behavior, voice chat content, or text.

Addiction and compulsive behavior are significant concerns, with excessive gaming leading to an inability to stop playing, even when it interferes with daily life. Signs include spending excessive time gaming, neglecting responsibilities, and experiencing withdrawal symptoms when not playing. Privacy and security issues also arise, as sharing personal information online can lead to privacy breaches and identity theft. Signs to watch for include unsolicited requests for personal information, suspicious friend requests, and unexpected changes in account settings.

Financial risks are another issue, as many games offer in-game purchases that can lead to unexpected expenses, especially if children have access to payment methods. Signs of this include unauthorized purchases, pressure to buy in-game items, and spending more than intended. Phishing and scams are common tactics used by cybercriminals to steal account information or money, often through emails or messages asking for login details or fake websites that mimic legitimate ones.

Downloading games or mods from unofficial sources can introduce malware and viruses to your device, leading to slow device performance, unexpected pop-ups, and unauthorized changes to system settings. Prolonged gaming can also negatively impact mental health, increasing stress, anxiety, and social isolation. Signs include feeling irritable or anxious when not playing, avoiding social interactions, and experiencing mood swings related to gaming. Additionally, online predators may use gaming platforms to exploit and manipulate younger players, with signs including unusual behavior from other players, requests to move conversations to private chats, and attempts to build trust quickly.

Strategies for Safe Online Gaming - To mitigate these risks, it's important to set boundaries and limits by establishing daily or weekly limits on gaming time and scheduling regular breaks to rest eyes and prevent physical strain. Enable privacy settings on gaming platforms to control who can contact you and view your profile, and restrict the sharing of personal information such as your real name, address, or phone number.

Monitor in-game purchases by using parental controls to restrict spending and setting strict spending limits. Be aware of cyberbullying by using reporting tools provided by gaming platforms to report abusive behavior and blocking players who engage in bullying or harassment. Educate yourself and others about the risks associated with online gaming and promote safe practices, such as not sharing personal information and being cautious with strangers.

Use security software like reputable antivirus and anti-malware programs to protect your device from threats, and keep your gaming software and devices updated with the latest security patches. Verify game sources by downloading games and mods only from official and trusted sources and checking reviews to ensure they are safe and reputable. Encourage balanced activities by promoting engagement in offline activities such as sports, hobbies, and social interactions, and maintaining a balanced lifestyle to ensure overall well-being.

While online gaming can be a fun and rewarding activity, it is essential to be aware of the potential risks and take steps to mitigate them. By setting boundaries, enabling privacy settings, monitoring purchases, and educating about online safety, you can ensure a safe and enjoyable gaming experience. Regularly review and update safety practices to stay ahead of emerging threats and maintain a balanced approach to digital and real-life activities.

CHAPTER XXXIX

Setting Boundaries and Safe Gaming Practices

Setting boundaries and practicing safe gaming habits are essential to ensure that online gaming remains a fun and healthy activity. These practices help prevent addiction, maintain physical and mental health, and protect against various online risks. Here are some strategies to establish boundaries and safe gaming practices.

Establishing Boundaries - Setting time limits is crucial. Determine how much time you or your child can spend on gaming each day or week and stick to these limits to prevent excessive gaming. Incorporate regular breaks during gaming sessions to rest your eyes and stretch your body, following the 20-20-20 rule: every 20 minutes, look at something 20 feet away for at least 20 seconds.

Designate gaming-free zones to promote healthier habits. Keep gaming consoles and computers out of bedrooms to encourage better sleep and avoid gaming during meals to foster family interactions and mindful eating. Balance gaming with other activities by engaging in physical exercise, such as sports, walking, or dancing, and dedicating time to offline hobbies and interests to ensure a well-rounded lifestyle.

Creating a gaming schedule can help maintain structure. Schedule specific times for gaming to prevent it from interfering with daily responsibilities like homework, chores, and social activities, and avoid long, uninterrupted gaming sessions by setting alarms or reminders to take breaks.

Safe Gaming Practices - Using privacy settings is essential. Adjust the privacy controls on gaming platforms to manage who can see your profile and contact you, and avoid sharing personal information like your real name, address, phone number, or financial details. Be aware of cyberbullying and harassment by recognizing signs such as offensive messages, targeting, and social exclusion. Use the reporting tools provided by gaming platforms to report abusive behavior and block players who engage in bullying or harassment.

Monitoring in-game purchases is crucial, especially for younger players. Enable parental controls to restrict spending and set strict spending limits if in-game purchases are allowed. Protect against phishing and scams by verifying the source of messages or emails asking for login details or financial information and using secure websites (look for "https" in the URL).

Ensure device security by installing reputable antivirus and anti-malware software and regularly updating your gaming software and devices with the latest security patches. Practice responsible gaming by being cautious when playing with strangers and limiting chat and messaging features to avoid uncomfortable or unsafe interactions.

Educate yourself and others about online safety by discussing the potential risks associated with online gaming and promoting safe practices, such as not sharing personal information and being cautious with strangers. Encourage healthy habits, including regular meals and proper hydration during gaming sessions, and maintain good posture and ergonomic setups to prevent physical strain and discomfort.

Parental Involvement - Parental involvement is vital in setting clear expectations for gaming. Establish rules for gaming and outline the consequences for not following them, maintaining open communication about gaming habits and encouraging discussions about any concerns. Monitor and guide your child's gaming activities by supervising the games they play and their online interactions. Occasionally play games with your child to understand their gaming world and promote safe practices.

Encourage offline social interactions by planning family activities that do not involve screens to strengthen family bonds and support your child in maintaining friendships and participating in social activities outside of gaming.

Setting boundaries and practicing safe gaming habits are essential for maintaining a healthy balance between digital and real-life activities. By establishing time limits, using privacy settings, being aware of online risks, and encouraging a balanced lifestyle, you can enjoy the benefits of gaming while minimizing its potential negative impacts. Regularly review and adjust these practices to ensure they continue to meet your needs and promote a safe and enjoyable gaming experience.

CHAPTER XL

Understanding In-Game Purchases and Scams

In-game purchases are a common feature in many online games, allowing players to buy virtual goods, enhancements, or currency. While these purchases can enhance the gaming experience, they also pose risks, including financial loss and exposure to scams. Understanding how in-game purchases work and how to avoid scams is crucial for a safe gaming experience.

In-game purchases come in various forms. Cosmetic items, such as skins, outfits, or emotes, change the appearance of characters or equipment but do not affect gameplay. Consumables provide temporary benefits like health potions, boosters, or extra lives. Permanent upgrades enhance a character's abilities or equipment permanently, while in-game currency, which can often be bought with real money, is used to purchase other in-game items or features. Payment methods for these purchases typically include credit/debit cards, digital wallets like PayPal or Apple Pay, and pre-paid gift cards specifically for the gaming platform. To prevent unauthorized spending, parents can enable controls to restrict or monitor in-game purchases and set spending limits.

Recognizing In-Game Scams - In-game scams can take several forms. Phishing scams involve scammers sending messages or emails pretending to be from the game company, asking for login details or financial information.

Signs include unsolicited messages or emails requesting personal information and links to websites that look similar to the game's official site but have slight differences in the URL. Another scam involves fake in-game items and currency, where scammers offer these at discounted rates outside the official game store, leading to financial loss and account compromise. Signs include offers that seem too good to be true and transactions requiring payment through unofficial channels.

Account theft is another risk, where scammers trick players into sharing their login credentials, leading to the loss of in-game progress and purchases. Signs include requests for account information, even from friends or trusted sources, and unusual activity or changes in account settings. Fake giveaways and contests are also common, where scammers promote these to lure players into providing personal information or downloading malicious software. Signs include contests or giveaways asking for personal information or payment and promises of high-value rewards with minimal effort.

Protecting Yourself from In-Game Scams - To protect yourself from in-game scams, always verify sources. Make purchases only through the game's official store or authorized platforms, ensuring the website URL is correct and starts with "https" for secure transactions. Enable two-factor authentication (2FA) on your gaming accounts to provide an extra layer of protection against unauthorized access. Be cautious with personal information by never sharing your login credentials and using strong, unique passwords. Educate yourself and others about common scams and safe practices, and discuss these risks with family members, especially younger players. Report any suspicious activity using in-game reporting tools and contact customer support if you believe you've been scammed.

For parents, setting up parental controls to restrict or require approval for in-game purchases and monitoring your child's gaming activity and purchase history is essential. Discuss spending habits with your child, teaching them about budgeting and the value of money to help them make informed decisions. Encourage responsible spending and explain the potential risks of in-game purchases. Play games with your child to understand the in-game purchase system and potential risks, and model safe online behavior and practices while gaming together.

In-game purchases can enhance the gaming experience, but they also come with risks, including financial loss and exposure to scams. By understanding how in-game purchases work, recognizing common scams, and following safe practices, you can protect yourself and your family from potential dangers. Regularly reviewing and updating your safety practices will help ensure a secure and enjoyable gaming experience.

Responsible Content Creation and Sharing

CHAPTER XLI

The Journey of Neha and Ravi

Neha and Ravi, two high school students from Bangalore, are passionate about content creation. Neha is a budding photographer who loves capturing moments and sharing them on Instagram. Ravi, on the other hand, runs a YouTube channel where he reviews tech gadgets and shares tips for young tech enthusiasts. Both are aware of the influence and reach they have online and are committed to creating and sharing content responsibly.

The Rise of Content Creators - Neha's Instagram feed is filled with stunning photographs of her city, capturing its vibrant culture and beautiful landscapes. She enjoys the creative process and the positive feedback she receives from her followers. However, she is also aware of the responsibilities that come with being a content creator.

Ravi's YouTube channel has gained a significant following. His reviews are thorough, and his tech tips are helpful to his audience. Ravi takes pride in his work and strives to maintain the integrity and quality of his content. He knows that his subscribers trust his opinions and recommendations.

The Challenge of Copyright and Intellectual Property - One day, Neha discovers that a popular page has reposted one of her photographs without giving her credit. She feels upset and frustrated, knowing that her hard work is being used without her permission. She decides to talk to her teacher, Mrs. Sharma, who teaches digital media at school.

Mrs. Sharma explains the importance of copyright and intellectual property rights. She advises Neha to watermark her photos and use platforms that protect creators' rights. She also encourages Neha to reach out to the page and request proper credit or removal of the photo.

Ethical Content Sharing -Ravi faces a different challenge. While researching for a new video, he comes across some information that he thinks would be perfect for his content. However, he realizes that using this information without proper attribution would be unethical. Ravi decides to dig deeper and find the original source of the information.

Ravi's friend, Sameer, suggests using content that is available under Creative Commons licenses, which allow creators to use, share, and build upon the work legally. Ravi takes this advice and ensures that he always credits the original creators when he uses their work. He also educates his viewers about the importance of respecting intellectual property rights.

Creating Positive and Impactful Content - Neha and Ravi are aware that their content can influence others. They decide to use their platforms to create positive and impactful content. Neha starts a project called "Faces of Bangalore," where she shares stories of ordinary people doing extraordinary things in her city. She ensures she has their permission to share their stories and photographs.

Ravi, inspired by Neha's project, decides to use his tech channel to promote digital literacy and online safety. He creates videos on topics like recognizing fake news, protecting personal information, and the importance of strong passwords. His goal is to educate his audience and help them navigate the digital world safely.

Engaging with the Community - Neha and Ravi also focus on engaging with their online communities responsibly. Neha responds to comments on her photos, thanking her followers and encouraging respectful discussions. She moderates her account to ensure it remains a positive space.

Ravi interacts with his subscribers by answering their questions and addressing their concerns in his videos. He promotes respectful communication and actively discourages any form of harassment or negativity on his channel.

Promoting Responsible Content Creation - Motivated by their experiences, Neha and Ravi decide to promote responsible content creation and sharing among their peers. They organize a seminar at their school, inviting other student content creators to share their stories and best practices.

During the seminar, Neha talks about the importance of respecting intellectual property rights and creating original content. Ravi discusses the ethics of content sharing and the impact of digital content on society. They also provide practical tips on creating positive and impactful content and engaging with online communities responsibly.

Neha and Ravi's story highlights the importance of responsible content creation and sharing. Their experiences underscore the need to respect intellectual property rights, create positive content, and engage with online communities ethically.

As we explore this chapter, we will delve deeper into the principles of responsible content creation and sharing, offering strategies and tools to help you become a conscientious and impactful content creator. By understanding and adopting these practices, you can contribute to a positive and respectful digital environment, just like Neha and Ravi.

CHAPTER XLII

Ethics of Sharing Content Online

Sharing content online has become an integral part of our digital lives. Whether it's posting on social media, blogging, or sharing videos, the ease of sharing information comes with ethical responsibilities. Understanding the ethical considerations of sharing content online is essential to maintaining a respectful, honest, and responsible digital environment.

Key Ethical Considerations - Accuracy and truthfulness are paramount when sharing content online. Always verify the accuracy of the information before sharing it, as spreading false or misleading information can have serious consequences. When sharing information from other sources, give proper credit to the original creators and provide references.

Respect for privacy is another critical consideration. Avoid sharing personal information about others without their consent, including names, addresses, phone numbers, and other sensitive details. Always obtain explicit permission before sharing someone else's photos, videos, or personal stories.

Adhering to copyright and intellectual property laws is essential. Do not share content that infringes on someone else's copyright; use content that you have created or have permission to share. Utilize content licensed under Creative Commons, ensuring you follow the terms of the license, such as attribution.

Consider the impact of your content on others. Think about the potential consequences of the content you share. Avoid sharing content that could harm someone's reputation, cause emotional distress, or incite violence. Do not engage in or support cyberbullying, and refrain from sharing content that humiliates, mocks, or targets individuals.

Cultural sensitivity is crucial in the diverse online environment. Be mindful of cultural differences and avoid sharing content that may be offensive or insensitive to other cultures. Use inclusive language and avoid stereotypes or derogatory terms.

Responsible sharing means avoiding sensationalism. Do not share content merely for shock value or to gain attention. Ensure the content has value and is shared responsibly. Promote content that fosters positivity, education, and constructive discussions.

Transparency and disclosure are vital. Clearly disclose if the content is sponsored or if you have received compensation for sharing it. Be authentic in your sharing, avoiding the creation or dissemination of content that misrepresents your identity or intentions.

Best Practices for Ethical Content Sharing - Thinking before you share is essential. Reflect on your intentions and consider why you are sharing the content and what you hope to achieve. Evaluate the potential impact of the content on your audience and the individuals involved.

Use reliable sources to verify information before sharing. Ensure that the information comes from credible sources and cross-check facts with multiple sources to confirm their accuracy.

Respect confidentiality by handling sensitive information with care and avoiding public sharing unless necessary and with permission. Do not share private conversations or messages without consent.

Engage constructively by aiming to contribute positively to online discussions. Avoid engaging in arguments or spreading negativity, and promote healthy and respectful dialogue, even when discussing controversial topics.

Educate yourself and others about ethical guidelines and best practices for sharing content online. Stay informed and raise awareness among your audience about the importance of ethical content sharing, encouraging them to adopt responsible practices.

Ethical Dilemmas and Challenges - Balancing freedom of expression and responsibility involves considering whether your content could harm others or spread misinformation. While you have the right to express yourself, strive to do so constructively and respectfully.

Dealing with misinformation requires taking responsibility for correcting false information if you realize you have shared it. Inform your audience and refrain from amplifying content that you suspect might be false or misleading.

Navigating anonymity means remembering that even when sharing content anonymously, you are accountable for the impact of your actions. Use anonymity responsibly and avoid using it to harm others or spread false information.

Ethical content sharing is about being responsible, respectful, and considerate of others. By following ethical guidelines and best practices, you can contribute to a positive and trustworthy online environment. Always think before you share, verify your information, and respect the privacy and rights of others. Engaging in ethical content sharing helps build a healthier and more respectful digital community.

CHAPTER XLIII

Understanding Copyright and Intellectual Property

Copyright and intellectual property (IP) laws protect the rights of creators and owners of original works. Understanding these concepts is essential for respecting the rights of others and ensuring your creations are protected. This guide covers the basics of copyright and intellectual property, their significance, and best practices for adhering to these laws.

What is Copyright? - Copyright is a legal right that grants the creator of an original work exclusive rights to its use and distribution, typically for a limited time. Protected works include literary, musical, and artistic creations such as books, music, paintings, sculptures, films, software, and architectural designs. Copyright grants several rights to the creator, including the right to reproduce, distribute, create derivative works, publicly perform, and display the work. Generally, copyright lasts for the life of the author plus 70 years after their death. For corporate, anonymous, and pseudonymous works, copyright lasts 95 years from publication or 120 years from creation, whichever is shorter.

What is Intellectual Property (IP)? - Intellectual property refers to creations of the mind, including inventions, literary and artistic works, designs, symbols, names, and images used in commerce. Types of IP include patents, which protect inventions and improvements; trademarks, which protect brand names, slogans, and logos; trade secrets, which protect confidential business information providing a competitive edge; and copyright, which protects original works of authorship. IP is crucial for providing economic incentives to creators and inventors, helping businesses differentiate their products and services, and offering legal recourse against unauthorized use or infringement.

Best Practices for Respecting Copyright and IP - When using copyrighted material, it is essential to seek permission from the copyright owner, which may involve licensing agreements or written consent. Understanding the fair use doctrine, which allows limited use of copyrighted material for purposes such as criticism, comment, news reporting, teaching, scholarship, or research, is also important. Utilizing works licensed under Creative Commons, which grants certain usage rights under specific conditions, can help you avoid infringement.

Always credit the creator when using someone else's work and follow the terms specified by the license under which the work is released. Creating and using your original content can help you avoid infringement issues, as can using works in the public domain whose copyrights have expired or whose creators have waived their rights. To protect your own IP, register your copyright, trademark, or patent to ensure you have legal protection and recourse against infringement. Adding watermarks, copyright notices, or other marks to your work can signal ownership and discourage unauthorized use.

Understanding Fair Use - Determining fair use involves

considering several factors: the purpose and character of the use (non-commercial, educational, or transformative use is more likely to be fair use); the nature of the work (using factual works is more likely to be fair use compared to highly creative works); the amount used (smaller portions are more likely to be fair use); and the effect on the market value of the original work (if the use does not significantly impact the market value, it is more likely to be fair use). Examples of fair use include educational use, criticism and commentary, and parody.

Consequences of Copyright Infringement - Copyright infringement can lead to legal consequences, including lawsuits where copyright holders can sue for damages and injunctions to stop further infringement. Courts may impose fines and order the infringer to pay damages. Infringement can also result in reputational damage, causing a loss of credibility and public relations issues that harm your public image.

Understanding and respecting copyright and intellectual property rights is essential for fostering a culture of creativity and innovation. By following best practices, such as seeking permission, providing proper attribution, and creating original content, you can avoid infringement issues and support the rights of creators. Protecting your own intellectual property also ensures that your creations are safeguarded and that you can benefit from your hard work.

CHAPTER XLIV

Creating Positive Digital Content

Creating positive digital content is essential for fostering a healthy, supportive, and enriching online environment. Positive content can inspire, educate, and uplift others while contributing to a more respectful and constructive digital community. Here are strategies for creating and sharing positive digital content.

Strategies for Creating Positive Digital Content - Focusing on constructive topics is a key strategy. Share educational content such as tutorials, how-to guides, and informative articles that help others learn and grow. Inspirational stories of resilience, success, and kindness can motivate and uplift your audience.

Promoting inclusivity and diversity ensures your content represents diverse voices and perspectives. Highlight stories from various cultural, social, and economic backgrounds, and use respectful, inclusive language for all people, regardless of gender, race, ethnicity, or ability.

Encouraging positive interactions by engaging respectfully with comments and messages is crucial. Respond with kindness, foster constructive discussions, and monitor content to remove any harmful or inappropriate comments.

Highlighting positive actions and initiatives such as community involvement, volunteering, and charitable efforts encourages others to participate in positive causes. Similarly, create content that promotes environmental sustainability and highlights efforts to protect the planet.

Providing support and resources through content that addresses mental health and well-being can be very impactful. Share articles on self-care, stress management, and where to seek help, along with content that empowers and motivates your audience to pursue their goals and overcome challenges.

Using visuals effectively can enhance the impact of your content. Positive imagery that evokes good emotions, combined with a clean and professional design, makes your content more appealing and engaging.

Sharing personal experiences adds authenticity. By discussing your personal stories and the lessons you've learned, you can connect with your audience on a deeper level, building trust and relatability.

Best Practices for Sharing Positive Digital Content - Verifying information is essential. Ensure the accuracy of the content you share and cite reliable sources to build credibility and trust with your audience.

Respecting privacy involves obtaining consent before sharing stories, photos, or videos of others, especially if the content is personal or sensitive. Protect personal information to avoid compromising anyone's privacy or security.

Being mindful of timing and sensitivity is crucial when addressing sensitive topics. Provide trigger warnings for potentially distressing content and approach these topics with care and consideration.

Encouraging feedback and interaction helps foster a sense of community. Invite your audience to share their thoughts, experiences, and feedback, and respond thoughtfully to show appreciation for their engagement.

Maintaining a positive tone involves steering clear of negativity and inflammatory language. Focus on positive and constructive communication, and highlight solutions and potential positive outcomes when discussing challenges or problems.

Examples of Positive Digital Content - Educational videos and tutorials, such as step-by-step guides on cooking, crafting, or technology, are valuable. Hosting informative webinars on educational topics can also benefit your audience.

Inspirational blog posts sharing success stories of individuals or organizations that have overcome challenges can be very motivating. Writing about personal growth journeys and the lessons learned along the way provides valuable insights.

Social media campaigns like hashtag challenges that encourage people to share their experiences or acts of kindness can create a ripple effect of positivity. Collaborations with other creators to promote positive messages and initiatives can further amplify your impact.

Podcasts and interviews featuring experts who share their insights and advice or guests who discuss their personal stories and experiences offer inspiration and motivation to your audience.

Creating positive digital content involves being intentional about the messages you share and the impact they have on your audience. By focusing on constructive topics, promoting inclusivity, encouraging positive interactions, and sharing authentic experiences, you can contribute to a more positive and supportive online environment. Always verify information, respect privacy, and maintain a positive tone to build trust and foster a healthy digital community.

Dealing with Misinformation and Fake News

CHAPTER XLV

Riya & A New Virus

In the bustling city of Mumbai, where the rich heritage of India blends seamlessly with modernity, Riya Patel, a diligent and curious 17-year-old student, navigates her academic life at one of the city's prestigious schools. Riya, like many of her peers, is highly active on social media, where she engages with friends, stays updated on current events, and explores various educational resources. However, the digital world is rife with misinformation and fake news, posing a significant challenge for young minds trying to discern the truth.

The Beginning of the Challenge - One Monday morning, Riya noticed a WhatsApp message from a school friend in their group chat. The message contained an alarming headline about a new virus outbreak in their city, supposedly more dangerous than anything seen before. The message included a link to a website with dubious claims and no credible sources. Her friend, in good faith, forwarded it to alert everyone.

Riya's initial reaction was fear and concern. Her classmates began discussing it frantically, sharing the message widely across various platforms. Within hours, it had spread to almost every student and parent group associated with the school. The school's principal, Mr. Sharma, had to address the growing panic among students and parents.

A Critical Lesson - In a special assembly, Mr. Sharma

emphasized the importance of verifying information before sharing it. He invited Mrs. Mehta, a respected journalist and Riya's media studies teacher, to educate the students about the dangers of fake news and the importance of media literacy.

Mrs. Mehta began by explaining the concept of fake news and misinformation, illustrating how easily false information can spread and cause unnecessary panic. She showed examples of past incidents where fake news had led to real-world consequences, emphasizing the need for skepticism and critical thinking.

Riya listened intently, realizing the gravity of the situation. Mrs. Mehta demonstrated tools and techniques for verifying information, such as checking the credibility of the sources, looking for multiple confirmations from reputable news outlets, and using fact-checking websites like Alt News and Factly.

The Investigation - Motivated by the assembly, Riya decided to investigate the viral message about the virus outbreak. She began by searching for news about it on credible news websites and found no reports confirming such an outbreak. Next, she used a reverse image search on the images included in the article and discovered they were taken from unrelated incidents from different parts of the world. She also found that the website hosting the article was known for spreading sensational fake news.

Armed with these findings, Riya shared her research with her friends in the WhatsApp group, debunking the viral message. She urged them to think critically before forwarding such alarming news and provided a list of reliable sources for health information, including the Ministry of Health and Family Welfare and the World

Health Organization.

Spreading Awareness - Riya's efforts didn't stop there. Recognizing the importance of combating misinformation, she proposed starting a "Media Literacy Club" at her school. With the support of Mrs. Mehta and Mr. Sharma, the club aimed to educate students about identifying fake news, verifying sources, and promoting digital literacy.

The club organized workshops, inviting experts to speak about various aspects of media literacy. They created posters and infographics to spread awareness and held regular discussions about current events, encouraging students to apply critical thinking and skepticism.

Impact and Reflection - Riya's initiative began to show positive results. Students became more cautious about the information they shared online, and the spread of fake news within their school community decreased significantly. The Media Literacy Club became a safe space for students to discuss their doubts and learn more about responsible online behavior.

Through this journey, Riya learned the importance of taking responsibility in the digital age. She understood that while the internet is a powerful tool for communication and learning, it requires a mindful and informed approach to navigate safely. Riya's proactive stance not only helped her peers but also inspired a culture of critical thinking and awareness in her school.

Riya's story is a testament to the power of education and proactive behavior in dealing with misinformation and fake news. It highlights how, with the right knowledge and tools, students can become responsible digital citizens, capable of discerning truth from falsehood and fostering a more informed and resilient community.

180

CHAPTER XLVI

Identifying Fake News and Misinformation

Fake news and misinformation are widespread in the digital age, posing risks to individuals and society by spreading false information and creating confusion. Identifying and mitigating fake news is crucial for maintaining an informed and accurate understanding of current events. Here are strategies for recognizing and combating fake news and misinformation.

Characteristics of Fake News and Misinformation - Fake news often features sensational headlines designed to attract attention and provoke emotional responses, often exaggerating or distorting facts. Phrases like "You Won't Believe," "Shocking," or "Unbelievable" are common indicators of sensationalism. Articles lacking credible sources or relying on unnamed sources or those with known biases are suspect. Additionally, frequent spelling and grammar mistakes or poorly designed websites with excessive ads and pop-ups can indicate a lack of professionalism and credibility.

Content that strongly appeals to emotions such as anger, fear, or joy may be designed to manipulate readers, and articles using divisive language to create conflict or target specific groups are red flags. Misinformation often includes bold claims without verifiable evidence or data and false statistics to support its assertions.

Strategies for Identifying Fake News and Misinformation - Verifying the source is essential. Research the credibility of the website or publisher, and look up the author to see if they are a reputable journalist or expert in the field. Cross-check information by verifying it with multiple credible sources, and use fact-checking websites such as Snopes, FactCheck.org, and PolitiFact to verify claims. Analyze the content by reading beyond the headline to understand the context and check for inconsistencies, and ensure the information is current and relevant. Recognize the potential bias of the source and the author, and look for articles that present multiple viewpoints and avoid one-sided narratives.

Evaluating visual content is also crucial. Use tools like Google Images for reverse searching images to see if they are taken out of context or misused, and analyze videos for signs of editing or manipulation. Apply critical thinking by asking questions about the information, such as who created it, why it was created, and what evidence supports it. Avoid confirmation bias by being open to information that challenges your beliefs and avoiding sharing information just because it aligns with your views.

Tools and Resources for Identifying Fake News - Fact-checking websites like Snopes, FactCheck.org, and PolitiFact are valuable resources for debunking myths, rumors, and misinformation. Browser extensions such as NewsGuard, which provides trust ratings for news websites, and Hoaxy, which visualizes the spread of claims and fact-checking online, can help users see how misinformation spreads. Reverse image search tools like Google Reverse Image Search and TinEye can verify the authenticity of images by showing where else they have appeared online. Educational platforms, including media literacy programs and online resources from organizations like the International Federation of Library Associations (IFLA), can teach how to critically analyze news and information.

Encouraging Responsible Sharing - Before sharing information, verify its accuracy and consider the potential impact of sharing false information. Promote media literacy by sharing tips and resources with friends and family to help them recognize fake news and encouraging others to approach news and information with skepticism and critical thinking. Support reliable sources by subscribing to and following news outlets known for their accuracy and reliability, and amplify accurate and verified information to help combat misinformation.

Identifying fake news and misinformation requires vigilance, critical thinking, and the use of reliable resources. By verifying sources, cross-checking information, and promoting media literacy, you can protect yourself and others from the harmful effects of misinformation. Responsible sharing and a commitment to accuracy are essential for maintaining an informed and truthful digital environment.

CHAPTER XLVII

Verifying Sources and Information

In the digital age, verifying sources and information is crucial to ensure the accuracy and credibility of the content you consume and share. With the proliferation of misinformation and fake news, having a critical approach to evaluating sources can help maintain the integrity of information. Here are effective strategies for verifying sources and information.

Steps to Verify Sources and Information - To verify the credibility of a source, start by researching its reputation. Established news organizations, academic institutions, and recognized experts are generally reliable. Ensure the source has expertise in the relevant field; authors and organizations should have credentials or a history of accurate reporting in the topic area. Transparency is another hallmark of credibility, so look for clear author attribution and organizational information.

Next, examine the author's background. Verify the author's qualifications and expertise related to the subject matter, review their previous work to see if they have a history of credible and accurate reporting, and check for any potential biases or affiliations that might influence their perspective.

Cross-checking information is vital. Verify the information by checking multiple reliable sources; consistency across various credible outlets indicates higher accuracy. Look for independent verification of claims, especially for significant or controversial information.

Evaluate the evidence presented in the article. Check if the article provides sources and citations for its claims, referencing studies, official reports, or direct quotes. Distinguish between primary sources (original data or firsthand accounts) and secondary sources (interpretations or summaries of primary data), with primary sources being generally more reliable.

Analyze the content itself. Ensure the information is current and relevant by checking the date of publication. Look for consistency in the facts presented; inconsistencies can be a red flag for misinformation. Assess the quality of writing; poor grammar, spelling mistakes, and unprofessional writing can indicate a lack of credibility.

Use fact-checking tools to assist in your verification. Websites like Snopes, FactCheck.org, and PolitiFact are invaluable for debunking myths and misinformation. Reverse image search tools like Google Reverse Image Search and TinEye can verify the authenticity of images and identify their origins.

Assess the website's credibility. Professional design, a reputable domain name, and the presence of an "About Us" section can indicate credibility. Be cautious of sites with excessive advertisements and pop-ups, and look for clear contact information, including physical addresses and phone numbers.

Check for bias by recognizing the potential bias of the source. All sources have some bias, but extreme bias can distort facts. Credible sources present multiple viewpoints and avoid overly one-sided narratives.

Tools and Resources for Verifying Sources - Fact-checking websites like Snopes, FactCheck.org, and PolitiFact are excellent resources for verifying claims and debunking misinformation. Reverse image search tools such as Google Reverse Image Search and TinEye help verify the authenticity of images. Browser extensions like NewsGuard, which provides trust ratings for news websites, and Hoaxy, which visualizes the spread of claims and fact-checking online, are also useful. Participating in media literacy programs and taking online courses on platforms like Coursera and edX can improve your ability to critically evaluate information.

Best Practices for Responsible Information Sharing - Before sharing information, verify its accuracy and consider the potential impact of sharing it. Avoid sharing content that could cause harm or spread misinformation. Encourage critical thinking by questioning sources and promoting skepticism towards sensational or too-good-to-be-true information. Educate yourself and others about the importance of verifying sources and the techniques to do so. Support reliable journalism by subscribing to and following news outlets known for their accuracy and integrity, and promote quality content by sharing accurate and well-researched information.

Verifying sources and information is essential for maintaining an informed and accurate understanding of the world. By critically evaluating sources, cross-checking information, and using reliable tools and resources, you can protect yourself and others from the harmful effects of misinformation. Responsible information sharing and a commitment to accuracy are vital for fostering a trustworthy digital environment.

CHAPTER XLVIII

The Role of AI in Spreading and Combating Misinformation

Artificial Intelligence (AI) plays a dual role in the realm of misinformation. On one hand, AI can be used to create and spread misinformation rapidly and efficiently. On the other hand, AI also offers powerful tools for detecting and combating misinformation. Understanding both aspects is crucial for developing effective strategies to mitigate the impact of false information.

AI in Spreading Misinformation - AI can significantly contribute to the spread of misinformation through automated content generation. Deepfakes, which are AI-generated videos and images that manipulate real footage to create realistic but fake content, can be used to spread false information by making it appear as though people said or did things they did not. Additionally, AI models like GPT-4 can generate large volumes of text that mimic human writing, creating convincing fake news articles, social media posts, and comments.

Social media bots further amplify misinformation. Automated accounts can post and share false information across social media platforms, making it appear more credible and widespread. Coordinated groups of bots, often referred to as troll farms, can engage in trolling activities to spread misinformation, disrupt conversations, and create division.

Microtargeting and personalization techniques also play a role in spreading misinformation. AI can analyze user data to deliver personalized ads that spread false information, targeting specific demographics and making the misinformation more effective and harder to detect. Additionally, AI-driven algorithms on social media platforms often promote content that aligns with users' existing beliefs, reinforcing echo chambers where misinformation can thrive.

AI in Combating Misinformation - AI also offers powerful tools for combating misinformation through automated fact-checking. AI-powered tools can analyze text in real-time to verify the accuracy of claims by cross-referencing them with reliable databases and flagging potential misinformation. AI can also scan articles, social media posts, and other content for signs of misinformation, such as the use of sensational language or lack of credible sources.

Image and video analysis are critical in detecting misinformation. AI algorithms can analyze videos and images to detect deepfakes by identifying inconsistencies and anomalies not visible to the human eye. Reverse image search tools help verify the authenticity of images by tracing their origins and identifying if they have been altered or used out of context.

AI can also identify bot activity through behavioral analysis. By analyzing patterns of behavior indicative of bot activity, such as rapid posting, repetitive comments, and coordinated amplification of content, AI can help identify fake accounts. Account verification techniques further assist in identifying fake accounts by examining profile details, activity patterns, and network connections.

Natural Language Processing (NLP) plays a crucial role in combating misinformation. Sentiment analysis can detect trends in misinformation and identify potentially harmful content by analyzing the sentiment of social media posts and articles. NLP algorithms can also classify content into categories such as fake news, clickbait, and credible information, helping platforms filter out misinformation.

User education and engagement are essential in combating misinformation. AI-powered education tools can create interactive platforms that teach users how to identify and combat misinformation, providing personalized feedback and resources. AI-driven bots can engage with users to provide accurate information and debunk myths in real-time, counteracting the spread of misinformation.

Challenges and Ethical Considerations - Despite its potential, AI in combating misinformation faces challenges and ethical considerations. AI tools are not infallible and can sometimes misidentify legitimate content as misinformation (false positives) or fail to detect actual misinformation (false negatives). AI algorithms can also inherit biases from their training data, leading to unequal treatment of different groups and perspectives.

Privacy concerns arise when combating misinformation requires analyzing large amounts of user data, raising issues about how this data is collected, stored, and used. Ensuring that AI tools are transparent in how they operate and make decisions is essential to maintaining user trust.

Misinformation tactics evolve rapidly, and AI systems must continuously adapt to new methods used by those spreading false information. Effective combating of misinformation often requires a combination of AI and human oversight to adapt to new challenges.

Best Practices for Using AI to Combat Misinformation - Collaborative efforts are crucial in combating misinformation. Partnerships between tech companies, governments, and independent fact-checkers can enhance the effectiveness of AI tools. Engaging users in the process of identifying and reporting misinformation can also improve AI accuracy and coverage.

Continuous improvement of AI systems is essential. Regularly updating AI algorithms to keep pace with new misinformation tactics and improving accuracy is crucial. Using diverse and comprehensive training data can reduce biases and enhance the reliability of AI tools.

Transparency and accountability in AI development are necessary. Implementing and communicating clear policies about how AI tools are used to combat misinformation, and providing mechanisms for users to report errors and give feedback, are essential for maintaining trust. Actively working to identify and mitigate biases in AI systems ensures fair and equitable treatment.

Ethical AI development prioritizes privacy protection. Developing AI tools that handle data responsibly and prioritize user privacy is crucial. Ensuring transparent operations and decision-making processes maintains user trust and fosters a trustworthy digital environment.

AI has a significant role in both spreading and combating misinformation. While it can be used to generate and amplify false information, it also provides powerful tools for detecting and countering misinformation. By understanding the dual role of AI and implementing best practices, we can leverage technology to create a more informed and trustworthy digital environment. Collaboration, continuous improvement, and ethical considerations are key to maximizing the positive impact of AI in the fight against misinformation.

Parental Guidance and Monitoring

CHAPTER XLIX

Rhea, Her Parents & Online Safety

Rhea, a 15-year-old student from Mumbai, loves spending time online. She uses social media to connect with friends, plays online games, and watches videos to learn new skills. While Rhea enjoys her digital life, her parents, Mr. and Mrs. Patel, are concerned about her online safety and the time she spends on her devices. This is the story of how they found a balance between trust, safety, and independence.

Rhea's parents understand the importance of digital literacy and want her to enjoy the benefits of the internet. However, they also worry about the potential risks such as cyberbullying, online predators, and exposure to inappropriate content. They want to ensure that Rhea is safe without making her feel like they are constantly watching over her shoulder.

Open Communication - One evening, the Patel family sits down for dinner. Mr. Patel initiates a conversation about online safety. He explains that they trust Rhea but want to discuss ways to keep her safe online. Rhea appreciates the open dialogue and feels comfortable sharing her online experiences with her parents.

Mrs. Patel suggests setting some ground rules for internet use. They agree to establish a few basic guidelines: Rhea should avoid sharing personal information, be cautious about accepting friend requests from strangers, and always inform her parents if she encounters anything that makes her uncomfortable.

To help monitor Rhea's online activity without being intrusive, Mr. Patel installs parental control software on Rhea's devices. He explains to Rhea that these tools are meant to protect her from potential threats and not to invade her privacy. Rhea understands and agrees to use the internet responsibly.

The parental control software allows Mr. Patel to set time limits on Rhea's device usage, block inappropriate content, and monitor the apps she downloads. He also sets up alerts for any unusual activity, ensuring that Rhea's online interactions are safe.

Educating About Online Risks - Mrs. Patel takes the time to educate Rhea about various online risks. They sit together and watch videos on cyberbullying, phishing scams, and the importance of maintaining strong passwords. Rhea learns about the significance of digital footprints and how to manage her online reputation.

Mrs. Patel also introduces Rhea to privacy settings on social media platforms, showing her how to control who can see her posts and how to report and block users who behave inappropriately.

Encouraging Responsible Digital Behavior - Rhea's parents encourage her to be a responsible digital citizen. They discuss the importance of treating others with respect online, just as she would in real life. Rhea learns about the impact of her words and actions on others and the importance of contributing positively to the online community.

To reinforce these values, Mr. and Mrs. Patel share their own experiences with technology and how they handle online interactions. This helps Rhea see the relevance of these lessons in everyday life.

As Rhea follows the agreed-upon guidelines and demonstrates responsible behavior online, her parents gradually give her more independence. They trust her to make the right decisions and are always there to support her if she needs help.

Rhea appreciates the trust her parents have in her and feels empowered to navigate the digital world safely. She becomes more confident in her ability to recognize and handle online threats, knowing that her parents are there to guide her when necessary.

Rhea and her parents' story highlights the importance of parental guidance and monitoring in ensuring online safety for teenagers. Their experience shows that open communication, education about online risks, and the use of parental controls can create a safe and supportive digital environment.

As we explore this chapter, we will delve into various strategies for parents to guide and monitor their children's online activities. By understanding and adopting these practices, parents can help their teens navigate the digital world safely and responsibly, just like Rhea and her parents.

CHAPTER L

Role of Parents in Ensuring Digital Safety

In today's digital age, children and teenagers are exposed to various online risks, including cyberbullying, inappropriate content, and privacy issues. Parents play a crucial role in ensuring their children's digital safety by educating them about responsible online behavior, setting appropriate boundaries, and monitoring their activities. Here are strategies for parents to help ensure digital safety for their children.

Educating Children About Digital Safety - Discussing online risks with children is essential. Parents should explain the potential dangers of the internet, such as cyberbullying, online predators, and exposure to inappropriate content, using age-appropriate language to ensure children understand the importance of digital safety. Teaching responsible online behavior is also vital. Emphasize the importance of treating others with respect and kindness online, just as they would in person, and encourage children to think carefully before sharing any personal information or posting content online. Promoting critical thinking is another key aspect. Teach children how to identify fake news and misinformation by checking sources and verifying facts, and encourage them to be skeptical of unsolicited messages and friend requests from strangers.

Setting Appropriate Boundaries - Establishing screen time limits helps maintain a healthy balance between online and offline activities. Set daily limits on screen time and create a consistent schedule that includes designated periods for homework, leisure, and family activities. Creating screen-free zones in certain areas of the home, such as the dining room and bedrooms, encourages face-to-face interactions, and setting a rule that all devices are turned off at least an hour before bedtime promotes better sleep hygiene. Using parental controls is another effective strategy. Implement content filters to block inappropriate websites and restrict access to age-inappropriate content, and utilize parental monitoring tools to keep track of your child's online activities and screen time.

Monitoring Online Activities - Regular check-ins with children about their online experiences help maintain open communication. Parents should actively ask about the websites their children visit and the people they interact with online, taking an active interest in their favorite games, apps, and social media platforms to better understand their online habits. Reviewing privacy settings on social media accounts and checking app permissions regularly can help protect children's personal information. Monitoring devices through shared accounts for younger children and periodically checking for unfamiliar apps or unusual activity can indicate inappropriate use or potential risks.

Encouraging Healthy Digital Habits - Modeling good behavior is crucial for parents. Demonstrate responsible digital behavior by adhering to the same rules and limits you set for your children, and show the importance of balancing screen time with other activities by engaging in offline hobbies and family activities. Promoting offline activities, such as physical exercise and participation in sports or outdoor games, helps maintain a balanced lifestyle. Support children's interests in offline hobbies like reading, drawing, or playing musical instruments. Fostering real-life social interactions by planning regular family activities that do not involve screens and encouraging children to spend time with friends in person helps build strong, healthy relationships.

Dealing with Digital Issues - Addressing cyberbullying involves recognizing signs, such as changes in behavior, reluctance to use devices, or distress after being online. If your child experiences cyberbullying, document the incidents and report them to the appropriate authorities, such as school officials or the platform where the bullying occurs. Handling inappropriate content requires an immediate response. Calmly discuss what your child saw and why it is inappropriate, and show them how to block and report inappropriate content or users on various platforms. Protecting personal information involves educating children about the importance of privacy and the potential consequences of oversharing. Encourage the use of strong, unique passwords for all online accounts and explain the importance of not sharing passwords with others.

Parents play a vital role in ensuring their children's digital safety. By educating children about online risks, setting appropriate boundaries, monitoring online activities, and encouraging healthy digital habits, parents can help their children navigate the digital world safely and responsibly.

Open communication and active involvement are key to fostering a safe and positive online environment for children.

CHAPTER LI

Tools and Techniques for Parental Control

In an increasingly digital world, parental control tools and techniques are essential for ensuring the online safety of children. These tools help parents monitor and manage their children's online activities, set appropriate boundaries, and protect them from potential online risks. Here are various tools and techniques for effective parental control.

Parental Control Tools - Built-in parental controls available in operating systems like Windows and macOS offer essential tools for managing children's online activities. These controls allow parents to set screen time limits, control app usage, and restrict access to certain websites. For instance, Windows provides Family Safety settings for time limits, content filters, and activity reporting, while macOS offers Screen Time settings with app limits and communication restrictions.

Mobile device controls are also crucial. On iOS devices, Apple's Screen Time feature enables parents to monitor usage, set app limits, and restrict content, with the ability to manage these settings remotely via Family Sharing. Similarly, Google's Family Link on Android devices allows parents to set screen time limits, approve or block apps, and monitor app activity, including setting daily device time limits.

Third-party parental control apps like Qustodio, Norton Family, and Net Nanny offer comprehensive monitoring solutions. Qustodio provides screen time limits, app usage tracking, web filtering, location tracking, and SOS alerts. Norton Family offers extensive content filtering, time management, and activity monitoring, including web supervision, search supervision, and video monitoring. Net Nanny is known for robust content filtering, screen time management, app blocking, and real-time alerts for inappropriate content.

Browser extensions such as uBlock Origin and BlockSite can enhance online safety by blocking ads, potential malware, and specific websites, and providing usage schedules and insights into browsing habits. Router-based controls like Circle with Disney and Netgear Nighthawk offer network-wide management. These devices allow for content filtering, time limits, device-specific controls, and pausing the internet for specific devices.

Techniques for Effective Parental Control - Setting clear boundaries and rules is fundamental. Parents should establish and communicate rules regarding Internet use, including acceptable websites, time limits, and consequences for breaking the rules, ensuring consistent enforcement to create a predictable and secure online environment.

Monitoring online activity involves regular check-ins to review a child's browsing history, app usage, and social media interactions. Parents should engage in open discussions about their children's online experiences, encouraging them to share both positive and negative encounters.

Educating children about online safety is crucial. Parents need to teach their children about the potential risks of the internet, such as cyberbullying, predators, and privacy issues, and encourage critical thinking about the information they encounter online to help identify fake news and misinformation.

Encouraging open communication creates a safe environment where children feel comfortable discussing their online experiences without fear of punishment. Active listening to their concerns and questions about online activities is essential for providing guidance and support.

Balancing online and offline activities helps maintain a healthy lifestyle. Parents should promote participation in offline activities such as sports, hobbies, and family time, and designate screen-free zones and times, like during meals or in bedrooms.

Using technology together allows parents to understand their children's interests and model good online behavior. Co-viewing websites, playing games, and watching videos together can also introduce children to educational resources and websites that provide valuable information and learning opportunities.

Addressing Specific Online Risks - Cyberbullying requires vigilance. Parents should recognize signs such as changes in behavior, reluctance to use devices, or distress after being online. Documenting incidents of cyberbullying and reporting them to relevant authorities, such as school officials or the platform where the bullying occurs, is essential.

Inappropriate content can be managed using content filtering tools to block access to unsuitable websites and apps. If a child encounters inappropriate content, parents should discuss why it is inappropriate and how to handle similar situations in the future.

Protecting privacy involves teaching children the importance of safeguarding their personal information online and the potential consequences of oversharing. Encouraging the use of strong, unique passwords for all online accounts and explaining the importance of not sharing passwords with others are key practices.

Dealing with online predators involves teaching children to recognize red flags, such as requests for personal information or attempts to move conversations to private channels. Children should be encouraged to report any suspicious behavior immediately so parents can take appropriate action to protect their safety.

Ensuring digital safety for children requires a combination of tools and techniques. By leveraging built-in parental controls, third-party apps, and router-based solutions, parents can effectively monitor and manage their children's online activities. Setting clear boundaries, educating about online safety, and encouraging open communication are crucial for fostering a safe and healthy digital environment. With these strategies, parents can help their children navigate the digital world safely and responsibly.

CHAPTER LII

Encouraging Open Communication

Open communication between parents and children is crucial for fostering a safe and supportive environment, especially in the context of digital safety. Encouraging open dialogue helps children feel comfortable sharing their online experiences, including any concerns or issues they encounter. Here are strategies for promoting open communication about digital safety.

Strategies for Encouraging Open Communication - Creating a safe and non-judgmental environment is essential. Parents should approach conversations with empathy and understanding, avoiding overly critical or punitive responses to their child's online activities. Active listening is also crucial—parents need to listen attentively to their child's concerns and questions, showing genuine interest in their experiences and validating their feelings.

Being approachable is another key aspect. Regularly check in with your child about their online activities by asking open-ended questions that encourage them to share more. Let them know that you are always available to talk and that they can come to you with any issues, no matter how small.

Leading by example helps reinforce responsible online behavior. Demonstrate respectful and responsible behavior online, as children are more likely to follow your example if they see you practicing what you preach. Share your own online experiences, including the challenges you face and how you handle them, to provide relatable guidance.

Educating together can make learning about digital safety more engaging. Explore digital safety topics together by watching videos, reading articles, and discussing what you learn. Stay informed about the latest digital trends and issues, and share this knowledge with your child to keep them aware and informed.

Discussing online risks openly is important for preparing your child to navigate the digital world. Clearly explain the potential risks associated with online activities, such as cyberbullying, privacy issues, and exposure to inappropriate content. Discuss hypothetical scenarios and how to handle them, which can help your child feel more prepared and confident in dealing with issues.

Encouraging critical thinking is another effective strategy. Teach your child to question the information they encounter online and discuss how to identify credible sources and recognize misinformation. Help them evaluate their online interactions and understand the importance of privacy and the potential consequences of sharing personal information.

Setting clear boundaries together can foster cooperation and understanding. Involve your child in setting rules for online behavior and screen time limits, making them feel more invested in following the rules. Clearly explain the reasons behind each rule so that your child understands the rationale and appreciates the importance of boundaries.

Addressing issues calmly and constructively helps maintain trust and encourages your child to come to you with problems. If your child comes to you with a problem, stay calm and avoid overreacting. Provide constructive feedback and solutions rather than punishment, focusing on learning and improvement.

Using technology together can strengthen your relationship and help you understand your child's online world. Spend time online together, watching videos, playing games, and exploring websites as a team. This shared experience can foster a deeper understanding and stronger connection. Introduce your child to educational resources that promote digital literacy and safety.

Celebrating positive online behavior reinforces good habits. Recognize and praise your child's positive online behavior, offering rewards and incentives for responsible actions and adherence to digital safety rules.

Addressing Specific Challenges - Dealing with cyberbullying requires vigilance and support. Be aware of signs of cyberbullying, such as changes in behavior, reluctance to use devices, or distress after being online. If your child is experiencing cyberbullying, provide emotional support and work together to address the issue, involving school officials or platform moderators if necessary.

Handling exposure to inappropriate content involves open discussion and guidance. If your child encounters inappropriate content, discuss it openly and calmly, explaining why the content is inappropriate and providing guidance on how to avoid it in the future. Show your child how to block and report inappropriate content or users on various platforms.

Navigating online privacy is critical for maintaining safety. Educate your child about the importance of protecting their personal information online, discussing privacy settings and the risks of oversharing. Encourage your child to share only what they are comfortable with and to think about the potential consequences of their online actions.

Encouraging open communication about digital safety involves creating a safe and supportive environment where children feel comfortable sharing their online experiences. By being approachable, leading by example, educating together, and addressing issues calmly, parents can foster a trusting relationship with their children. Open dialogue, combined with critical thinking and collaborative rule-setting, helps children navigate the digital world safely and responsibly.

Legal Aspects of Digital Safety

CHAPTER LIII

Ananya and her Cyber Law Project

Ananya, a 17-year-old student from Delhi, had always been passionate about technology. She loved exploring new apps and platforms, and she was particularly interested in how the internet worked. Her school offered a special project for students interested in law and technology, and Ananya jumped at the opportunity. This is the story of how Ananya discovered the importance of understanding the legal aspects of digital safety.

The Introduction to Cyber Laws - One day, during her computer science class, Ananya's teacher, Mr. Rao, announced a new project. Students would research and present on various aspects of cyber laws in India. Ananya was excited and chose to focus on laws protecting teenagers online. She wanted to understand how the legal system safeguarded young internet users like her.

Mr. Rao provided the students with a list of resources, including websites of government agencies, legal documents, and news articles. Ananya dived into her research with enthusiasm.

Understanding Cybercrimes and Laws - As Ananya delved into her project, she learned about the Information Technology Act, 2000, which was the primary law in India dealing with cybercrimes and electronic commerce. She was fascinated by the different sections of the act that dealt with issues like hacking, identity theft, and cyberbullying.

Ananya also discovered the role of the Cyber Crime Investigation Cell and how it worked to address online crimes. She was particularly interested in how the law protected minors from online predators and scams. She read case studies and legal reports, which gave her a deeper understanding of the practical applications of these laws.

During this time, an incident occurred at Ananya's school that brought her research to life. One of her classmates, Rohan, became a victim of cyberbullying. Someone created a fake social media profile using Rohan's name and posted hurtful comments. Rohan was devastated and didn't know what to do.

Ananya approached Mr. Rao and suggested that they use this incident as a learning opportunity. With Rohan's permission, they decided to discuss the situation in class and educate everyone about the legal steps they could take.

Taking Legal Action - With Mr. Rao's guidance, Ananya and Rohan reported the incident to the school authorities. The school's counselor contacted the Cyber Crime Investigation Cell. An officer visited the school and explained the process of filing a complaint and how the law would address the issue.

Ananya was impressed by the swift response. The fake profile was taken down, and the authorities traced the perpetrator. Rohan received support from his friends and teachers, and the incident became a powerful lesson for the entire school on the importance of digital safety and the effectiveness of cyber laws.

Creating Awareness - Inspired by her experience, Ananya decided to create an awareness campaign in her school. She and her classmates organized workshops where they discussed various cybercrimes, the legal protections available, and the importance of reporting incidents.

Ananya created a presentation that included real-life examples, important sections of the IT Act, and tips on how to stay safe online. She emphasized the importance of strong passwords, recognizing phishing attempts, and the need to report any suspicious activities.

Empowering Students - The campaign was a huge success. Students appreciated the practical information and felt more empowered to protect themselves online. Ananya's efforts were recognized by the school, and she was invited to present her project at an inter-school competition.

In her presentation, Ananya highlighted the importance of understanding cyber laws and how they protected individuals. She shared Rohan's story (with his permission) as a case study, demonstrating how legal measures could effectively address and resolve cybercrimes.

Ananya's story illustrates the significance of understanding the legal aspects of digital safety. Her journey from research to real-life application underscores the importance of awareness and education in protecting oneself online.

As we explore this chapter, we will delve deeper into the legal framework that governs digital safety in India. By understanding these laws and knowing how to use them, you can protect yourself and others from online threats, just like Ananya and her classmates.

CHAPTER LIV

Understanding Indian Cyber Laws

Indian cyber laws are designed to regulate activities in cyberspace and ensure the protection of digital information and the security of online transactions. With the increasing reliance on digital platforms, understanding these laws is essential for individuals, businesses, and organizations to operate legally and securely in the digital environment.

Key Indian Cyber Laws - The Information Technology Act, 2000 (IT Act) is the primary legislation governing cyber activities in India. It provides legal recognition to electronic transactions, digital signatures, and electronic records. The IT Act was amended in 2008 to address new challenges and strengthen the legal framework for cybersecurity.

Key provisions of the IT Act include the legal recognition of digital signatures and the establishment of the Controller of Certifying Authorities (CCA) to regulate certifying authorities. The Act also includes provisions for electronic governance, granting legal recognition to electronic records and signatures for government transactions. It addresses various cybercrimes, such as hacking, identity theft, cyberstalking, and the spread of malware, and sets rules for protecting sensitive personal data, requiring companies to implement reasonable security practices.

Important sections of the IT Act include Section 43, which penalizes unauthorized access, downloading, and damage to computer systems and data, and Section 66, which addresses hacking and related offenses. Section 66A, which dealt with offensive messages through communication services, was struck down by the Supreme Court in 2015. Section 67 penalizes the publishing or transmitting of obscene content in electronic form, while Section 69 grants the government powers to intercept, monitor, or decrypt information for security purposes. Section 72 imposes penalties for breaches of confidentiality and privacy.

The Indian Penal Code (IPC) also includes provisions related to cybercrimes. Sections 463-471 deal with forgery, applicable to digital documents, while Sections 383-389 address extortion, including cyber extortion and ransomware. Sections 499-502 cover defamation, applicable to online defamation.

Other relevant legislation includes the Personal Data Protection Bill, 2019, a proposed law aimed at protecting personal data and regulating its processing, which will replace existing data protection provisions under the IT Act once enacted. The National Cyber Security Policy, 2013, outlines strategies for protecting national cyberspace and critical information infrastructure.

Cyber Crimes and Legal Consequences - Cybercrimes such as hacking and unauthorized access involve gaining unauthorized access to computer systems or networks to steal, alter, or destroy data. Legal consequences under Sections 43 and 66 of the IT Act include fines and imprisonment.

Identity theft and fraud involve stealing personal information to commit fraud or deception. Legal consequences include penalties under Section 66C of the IT Act and relevant sections of the IPC.

Cyberstalking and harassment involve using electronic communication to stalk, harass, or intimidate individuals. Legal consequences include penalties under other sections of the IT Act and IPC since Section 66A was struck down.

Online defamation involves publishing false statements online that harm an individual's reputation. Legal consequences include penalties under Sections 499-502 of the IPC.

Distribution of obscene content involves publishing, transmitting, or creating obscene content online, with penalties under Section 67 of the IT Act.

Cyber terrorism involves using cyber tools to threaten national security or cause widespread disruption, with penalties under Section 66F of the IT Act, including life imprisonment.

Data Protection and Privacy - Under the IT Act, data protection rules require companies to implement reasonable security practices to protect sensitive personal data and obtain explicit consent for collecting such data. There is also an obligation to report data breaches to affected individuals and authorities.

The proposed Personal Data Protection Bill, 2019, defines roles and responsibilities for entities processing personal data and outlines data subject rights, including access, correction, and erasure of personal data. It also includes data localization requirements for storing certain categories of personal data within India and imposes significant penalties for non-compliance with data protection requirements.

Cyber Law Enforcement and Regulatory Bodies - Cybercrime investigation units include state cyber cells, each state having specialized units to investigate and address cybercrimes, and the Central Bureau of Investigation (CBI), which has a dedicated Cyber Crime Investigation Cell.

Regulatory authorities include the Ministry of Electronics and Information Technology (MeitY), responsible for formulating and implementing policies related to information technology, and the Indian Computer Emergency Response Team (CERT-In), the national agency responsible for responding to cybersecurity incidents and providing guidelines for information security.

The judicial framework includes adjudicating officers designated under the IT Act to handle disputes and complaints related to cybercrimes and breaches, and the Cyber Appellate Tribunal, an appellate body to hear appeals against decisions of the adjudicating officers.

Best Practices for Compliance and Protection - To comply with Indian cyber laws and protect against cyber threats, implement strong security measures, such as regular software updates and strict access controls. Educate employees and users through training programs and awareness campaigns on cybersecurity best practices and data protection.

Develop comprehensive data protection and privacy policies, conduct regular security audits and risk assessments, and implement an incident response plan to handle cybersecurity incidents effectively. Establish clear communication channels for reporting and addressing security breaches.

Understanding Indian cyber laws is essential for navigating

the digital landscape legally and securely. By familiarizing yourself with the key provisions of the IT Act, other relevant legislation, and best practices for compliance, you can protect yourself and your organization from cyber threats and legal consequences. Staying informed and proactive about cybersecurity measures and legal requirements is crucial in today's interconnected world.

CHAPTER LV

Legal Rights and Responsibilities for Teens

As teenagers navigate their way through adolescence, they gain certain legal rights and responsibilities. Understanding these rights and responsibilities helps teens make informed decisions and understand the legal implications of their actions. This guide provides an overview of key legal rights and responsibilities for teens in India.

Legal Rights of Teens - Teens in India are guaranteed the right to education under the Right to Free and Compulsory Education Act, 2009 (RTE Act), which ensures free and compulsory education for all children aged 6 to 14 years. Additionally, under the Information Technology Act, 2000 (IT Act), they have the right to privacy, which includes protection against unauthorized use of personal data and cyberbullying. Teens also have the right to personal privacy, encompassing the confidentiality of their personal information and communication.

The Child Labour (Prohibition and Regulation) Act, 1986 prohibits the employment of children under 14 years in hazardous occupations and regulates their working conditions in non-hazardous occupations. The Protection of Children from Sexual Offences Act, 2012 (POCSO Act) provides legal protection from sexual abuse and exploitation. Teens have the right to participate in decisions affecting their lives, including educational and healthcare decisions, and the right to be heard is recognized under various international conventions, allowing them to express their views and opinions. Furthermore, teens have the right to free speech and freedom of expression, provided they do not infringe on others' rights or violate laws against hate speech and defamation.

Legal Responsibilities of Teens - Teens must obey the law, including laws related to cyber conduct, substance use, and public behavior. They should understand the potential legal consequences of unlawful actions, such as fines, community service, or juvenile detention. Respecting digital privacy is essential; teens must refrain from cyberbullying, hacking, or unauthorized data sharing and avoid illegal downloading or sharing of copyrighted material.

School attendance and conduct are also responsibilities for teens. They must attend school regularly and complete their education as mandated by the RTE Act, adhering to school rules and regulations related to behavior, academic integrity, and dress code. Respecting others' rights is crucial; teens must avoid discriminatory behavior based on race, gender, religion, or any other characteristic and refrain from all forms of bullying, harassment, and violence, both online and offline.

Teens must also adhere to laws that prohibit the use, possession, and distribution of alcohol and drugs for individuals under the legal age. They are encouraged to participate positively in their communities, volunteer, contribute to social causes, and engage in sustainable practices to protect the environment.

Key Legal Ages in India - The age of majority in India is 18 years, at which point a person is considered an adult in the eyes of the law and gains full legal capacity to enter into contracts, vote, and marry without parental consent. The driving age is set at 16 years for obtaining a learner's permit for a motorcycle without gear and 18 years for a car or motorcycle with gear. The minimum age for employment in non-hazardous industries is 14 years, while it is 18 years for hazardous industries. The legal age of consent for sexual activity, as stipulated by the POCSO Act, is 18 years. For marriage, the legal minimum age is 18 years for women and 21 years for men.

Legal Support and Resources - Legal aid and counseling are available through the National Legal Services Authority (NALSA), which provides free legal aid to those in need, including teens. Childline (1098) is a 24/7 helpline for children in distress, offering support and intervention. Educational resources such as school programs and workshops on legal rights and responsibilities are often provided, along with online resources that offer information and guidance on legal matters for teens. Various non-governmental organizations (NGOs) work towards educating and protecting the rights of children and teens, while community support groups provide counseling and assistance to teens facing legal or social issues.

Understanding their legal rights and responsibilities helps teens navigate their way through adolescence with confidence and awareness. By being informed about the laws that protect and govern them, teens can make better decisions and avoid legal pitfalls. Parents, educators, and communities play a crucial role in providing guidance and support to help teens understand and fulfill their legal responsibilities while exercising their rights.

CHAPTER LVI

Reporting Cybercrimes

Cybercrimes, including hacking, identity theft, cyberbullying, and online fraud, are increasingly common in today's digital world. Reporting these crimes is crucial for obtaining justice, protecting oneself, and preventing future incidents. This guide outlines the steps for reporting cybercrimes in India, the authorities involved, and tips for ensuring a comprehensive and effective report.

Steps for Reporting Cybercrimes - The first step in reporting a cybercrime is to document the evidence. Gather all relevant information, such as screenshots, emails, chat logs, and any other digital evidence that can support your case. It is essential to keep the original copies of evidence intact and avoid modifying, deleting, or tampering with the evidence. Next, identify the nature of the cybercrime you are dealing with, whether it is hacking, phishing, identity theft, cyberbullying, or online fraud. Familiarize yourself with the legal definitions and provisions related to the cybercrime under the Information Technology Act, 2000, and other relevant laws.

Once you have documented the evidence and identified the nature of the crime, report it to the appropriate authorities. Visit your nearest police station to file a First Information Report (FIR) and provide all collected evidence and a detailed account of the incident. Many cities have dedicated cybercrime cells or units specializing in handling cybercrimes, and reporting directly to these units can expedite the process. Additionally, the Government of

India has launched the National Cyber Crime Reporting Portal (www.cybercrime.gov.in), where individuals can report cybercrimes online. Visit the portal, select the type of cybercrime, fill in the required details, upload evidence, and submit the report. After submitting the report, you will receive a tracking number to monitor the status of your complaint.

You can also report cyber crimes to specialized agencies such as the Indian Computer Emergency Response Team (CERT-In), the national nodal agency for responding to cybersecurity incidents. Reports can be made via email (incident@cert-in.org.in) or through their website (www.cert-in.org.in). For broader issues related to digital security and policies, you can contact the Ministry of Electronics and Information Technology (MeitY). If the cybercrime involves financial fraud or identity theft, notify your bank or financial institution immediately and request them to freeze accounts or transactions if necessary. Report the incident to the relevant online platform or service provider, such as social media sites, email providers, or e-commerce websites, as they may have specific procedures for handling such incidents.

Authorities Involved in Handling Cybercrimes - The first point of contact for reporting cybercrimes is the local police station, where you can file an FIR and initiate an investigation. Some police departments have specialized cybercrime units equipped with trained personnel and advanced tools for dealing with digital evidence and cyber forensic analysis. The Central Bureau of Investigation (CBI) also has a Cyber Crime Investigation Cell that handles high-profile and complex cybercrime cases, often involving inter-state or international elements. CERT-In coordinates responses to cybersecurity incidents and provides guidance on best practices for prevention and mitigation. The National Cyber Crime Reporting Portal facilitates the reporting of cybercrimes through a user-friendly online portal.

Tips for Effective Reporting - When reporting a cybercrime, it is essential to be detailed and specific. Provide a comprehensive description of the incident, including dates, times, and all relevant details, ensuring your report is clear and concise. Approach the reporting process calmly and cooperatively, understanding that investigations take time. Be prepared to answer questions, provide additional information, and cooperate with the investigation. Use the tracking number provided by the reporting portal or follow up with the authorities to check the status of your complaint, stay informed about the progress of the investigation, and being responsive to any requests from the authorities.

To protect your information, change your passwords immediately and enable two-factor authentication (2FA) if your accounts have been compromised. Regularly monitor your financial and online accounts for any unusual activity. Consider consulting a lawyer who specializes in cyber law to guide you through the reporting process and protect your legal rights.

Reporting cybercrimes is essential for obtaining justice and preventing further incidents. By following the steps outlined above, documenting evidence, and cooperating with the authorities, individuals can effectively report cybercrimes and contribute to a safer digital environment. Staying informed about legal rights and responsibilities, as well as utilizing available resources and support, is crucial in navigating the complexities of cybercrime reporting.

AI and the Future of Digital Safety

CHAPTER LVII

Arjun and His Tech Project

Arjun, a 16-year-old student from Bangalore, was known for his curiosity about technology. He spent his free time reading about the latest advancements and tinkering with gadgets. When his school announced a tech fair, Arjun decided to take on an ambitious project that combined his interests in artificial intelligence (AI) and digital safety. This is the story of how Arjun explored the potential of AI in enhancing digital safety for the future.

Choosing the Project- Arjun's school encouraged students to come up with innovative ideas for the tech fair. The theme for this year was "The Future of Technology." Arjun immediately thought about AI and its impact on digital safety. He had read about how AI was being used to detect online threats, prevent cyberattacks, and protect personal data.

With the help of his computer science teacher, Mrs. Iyer, Arjun decided to create a project that demonstrated how AI could enhance digital safety for teenagers. He wanted to show his peers how AI could be their ally in navigating the digital world safely.

Arjun started his project by researching various AI technologies used in cybersecurity. He learned about machine learning algorithms that could detect unusual patterns in online behavior, AI-powered tools that identified phishing emails, and chatbots designed to provide real-time assistance for online safety.

Inspired by these applications, Arjun decided to develop a prototype of an AI-based digital safety assistant for teenagers. He envisioned it as a mobile app that could monitor online activities, provide safety tips, and alert users to potential threats.

Building the Prototype - Arjun spent weeks coding and testing his prototype. He used open-source machine learning libraries and trained his model on datasets that included examples of safe and unsafe online behavior. Mrs. Iyer helped him refine the algorithm to improve its accuracy.

The prototype, which Arjun named "SafeNet," could analyze a user's social media interactions, flag suspicious messages, and suggest actions to enhance privacy settings. It also included a feature where users could ask questions about digital safety and receive AI-generated advice.

The Tech Fair Presentation -The day of the tech fair arrived, and Arjun was excited to present SafeNet. He set up his booth with posters explaining how AI worked, the importance of digital safety, and the features of his app. He also had a live demo of SafeNet to showcase its capabilities.

As students, teachers, and parents visited his booth, Arjun explained how SafeNet could help them stay safe online. He demonstrated how the app could detect phishing attempts, advise on creating strong passwords, and monitor for signs of cyberbullying.

Real-Life Application - During the tech fair, a student named Kavya approached Arjun. She shared her experience of receiving a suspicious message from an unknown number. Kavya had ignored the message, but it made her anxious about her online safety.

Arjun used SafeNet to analyze the message Kavya received. The app flagged it as a potential phishing attempt and suggested blocking the number and reporting it. Kavya was impressed by the app's ability to provide immediate guidance and felt more confident in handling similar situations in the future.

Recognition and Future Plans

Arjun's project received widespread appreciation at the tech fair. Teachers and students were impressed by the practical application of AI in enhancing digital safety. Arjun won the "Best Innovative Project" award, and his school decided to support him in developing SafeNet further.

Inspired by the positive feedback, Arjun envisioned expanding SafeNet to include more features, such as AI-driven parental controls and tools to help teachers monitor digital safety in schools. He also planned to collaborate with cybersecurity experts to refine the app's algorithms and make it available to a broader audience.

Arjun's story highlights the transformative potential of AI in the realm of digital safety. His project not only showcased the power of AI but also educated his peers on how technology could be harnessed to create a safer online environment.

As we explore this chapter, we will delve into how AI is shaping the future of digital safety. By understanding these advancements, we can prepare ourselves to navigate the digital world more securely, just like Arjun and his innovative approach with SafeNet.

CHAPTER LVIII

Emerging AI Technologies and Their Impact

Artificial Intelligence (AI) is rapidly evolving, bringing transformative changes across various sectors. Emerging AI technologies are reshaping industries, enhancing productivity, and introducing new capabilities that were once the realm of science fiction. This guide explores some of the latest AI technologies and their potential impacts on society, the economy, and individual lives.

Key Emerging AI Technologies - Natural Language Processing (NLP) involves the interaction between computers and humans using natural language. Recent advancements include more sophisticated language models that understand, interpret, and generate human language with high accuracy. Applications of NLP include chatbots and virtual assistants for enhanced customer service and user interaction, automated content creation such as generating articles and reports, and improved real-time translation services.

Computer vision enables machines to interpret and make decisions based on visual data. It includes image recognition, object detection, and facial recognition technologies. Applications in healthcare involve improved diagnostics through medical imaging analysis, enhanced surveillance and facial recognition for security purposes, and automated checkout systems and inventory management in retail.

Machine learning (ML) and deep learning (DL) are subsets of AI where machines learn from data to make predictions or decisions. Deep learning involves neural networks with many layers that analyze complex patterns. In finance, these technologies are used for fraud detection and algorithmic trading. In healthcare, they enable predictive analytics for disease outbreaks and personalized medicine, while in marketing, they help with customer segmentation and personalized recommendations.

Robotic Process Automation (RPA) uses software robots to automate repetitive and rule-based tasks traditionally performed by humans. Applications include automated data entry and reconciliation in finance, handling routine inquiries and processing transactions in customer service, and automating recruitment and onboarding processes in human resources.

Autonomous systems include self-driving cars, drones, and robotic systems capable of performing tasks without human intervention. Applications range from autonomous vehicles for personal and public transport to drones for package delivery and automated production lines with robotic assembly in manufacturing.

Generative Adversarial Networks (GANs) are AI algorithms used to generate new data samples that resemble a given dataset. They consist of two neural networks, a generator and a discriminator, that work together to produce realistic outputs. GANs are used in art and design to create realistic images and music, in data augmentation to generate synthetic data for training AI models, and in entertainment to enhance special effects and create virtual characters.

Impact of Emerging AI Technologies - AI technologies can significantly enhance productivity by automating repetitive tasks, optimizing operations, and improving decision-making processes. While AI can create new job opportunities in tech and data fields, it may also displace certain roles, particularly those involving routine tasks. Reskilling and upskilling the workforce will be crucial.

In healthcare, AI can analyze medical data to provide accurate diagnoses, predict disease outbreaks, and personalize treatment plans, leading to better patient outcomes. Automating administrative tasks and streamlining workflows in healthcare institutions can reduce costs and enhance patient care.

AI-driven insights can help businesses offer personalized recommendations and services, improving customer satisfaction and loyalty. Chatbots and virtual assistants provide round-the-clock customer support, enhancing user experience and efficiency.

AI-powered surveillance systems can detect suspicious activities and potential threats more accurately and promptly. AI can also help identify and mitigate cybersecurity threats, safeguarding sensitive information.

AI systems can inadvertently perpetuate biases present in training data, leading to unfair outcomes. Ensuring fairness and transparency in AI systems is essential. The extensive data collection required for AI applications raises concerns about user privacy. Robust data protection measures and regulations are necessary. The deployment of AI in areas like surveillance and autonomous weapons raises ethical questions about privacy, security, and accountability.

AI can optimize energy consumption and resource management, contributing to sustainability efforts. AI technologies can enhance environmental monitoring and predict natural disasters, aiding in disaster preparedness and response.

Preparing for the Future with AI - Emphasizing science, technology, engineering, and mathematics (STEM) education prepares the future workforce for AI-related careers. Encouraging continuous learning and professional development keeps pace with AI advancements and evolving job requirements.

Developing and implementing policies and regulations ensure the ethical use of AI and protect individual rights. Fostering international cooperation addresses. global challenges related to AI, such as cybersecurity and ethical standards.

Supporting AI research and innovation drives technological advancements and maintains competitive advantage. Encouraging collaboration between the public and private sectors leverages resources and expertise for AI development.

Implementing strategies to identify and mitigate biases in AI systems ensures fair and equitable treatment. Ensuring AI systems are transparent and accountable, with clear mechanisms for addressing grievances and errors, fosters trust and reliability.

Emerging AI technologies are poised to transform various aspects of our lives, from improving healthcare and enhancing customer experiences to driving economic growth and addressing environmental challenges. However, the widespread adoption of AI also brings significant ethical, social, and regulatory challenges. By fostering a balanced approach that promotes innovation while addressing these challenges, society can harness the full potential of AI for the greater good.

CHAPTER LIX

Preparing for Future Digital Challenges

The rapid advancement of digital technologies brings both opportunities and challenges. As society becomes increasingly dependent on digital platforms, it's crucial to prepare for future digital challenges. This guide explores key strategies for individuals, businesses, and governments to effectively navigate and thrive in an evolving digital landscape.

Key Areas to Focus On - Cybersecurity is a top priority in the digital age. Enhancing security measures such as firewalls, encryption, and multi-factor authentication is essential for protecting against cyber threats. Regular updates and patches are necessary to keep software and systems secure from vulnerabilities. Cyber hygiene education is also crucial, as it equips individuals and employees with the knowledge to recognize phishing attempts and maintain strong, unique passwords.

Digital literacy and skills development are critical for preparing for future digital challenges. Promoting digital literacy ensures that people of all ages understand basic digital skills and online safety. Continuous learning through training programs helps individuals and employees stay current with emerging technologies. Emphasizing science, technology, engineering, and mathematics (STEM) education builds a workforce capable of leveraging advanced technologies.

Data privacy and protection are fundamental in the digital era. Implementing data protection policies that comply with local and international regulations is essential. Maintaining transparency about data collection, storage, and usage, and giving individuals control over their personal data, is vital. Data minimization practices, which involve collecting only the necessary data for specific purposes and storing it securely, also play a key role.

Ethical AI and automation are crucial areas of focus. Identifying and mitigating biases in AI systems ensures fair and equitable outcomes. Developing AI systems that are transparent and accountable, with clear mechanisms for addressing errors and grievances, is important. Establishing ethical guidelines for AI development and use is necessary to ensure these technologies benefit society.

Regulatory and policy frameworks must evolve to address the challenges posed by digital technologies. Governments should develop comprehensive policies covering cybersecurity, data privacy, and AI ethics. International collaboration is essential for creating global standards and regulations. Public-private partnerships can leverage expertise and resources from both sectors for effective digital governance.

Resilience against disinformation requires promoting media literacy to help the public critically evaluate information sources and recognize misinformation. Supporting fact-checking organizations and initiatives is crucial for providing accurate information and debunking false claims. Transparent communication from official sources enhances public trust and ensures accessible, credible information.

Innovation and adaptability are key to thriving in the digital landscape. Supporting research and development drives innovation and maintains competitive advantage. Encouraging businesses to adopt flexible and adaptable business models allows them to respond quickly to technological changes and market demands. Creating an environment that supports startups and entrepreneurs fosters innovative digital solutions.

Practical Steps for Individuals - Staying informed about digital trends and cybersecurity is crucial. Regularly reading articles, attending webinars, and participating in forums can help individuals keep up with the latest developments. Networking with experts through professional groups can provide valuable insights and connections.

Improving personal cybersecurity is essential. Using strong, unique passwords for all accounts and utilizing a password manager enhances security. Enabling two-factor authentication adds an extra layer of protection to online accounts. Being cautious online, such as avoiding suspicious links and unsolicited messages, reduces the risk of cyber threats.

Enhancing digital skills through online courses and certifications helps individuals stay competitive in the digital age. Gaining practical experience through projects, internships, or volunteer work in the tech field can also be beneficial.

Strategies for Businesses - Investing in cybersecurity is a priority for businesses. Establishing a dedicated cybersecurity team to monitor, manage, and respond to threats is crucial. Conducting regular security audits and vulnerability assessments helps identify and address potential risks.

Fostering a culture of continuous learning within the organization is important. Providing regular training sessions on cybersecurity, data protection, and emerging technologies keeps employees informed and prepared. Encouraging participation in innovation programs and hackathons can inspire new ideas and solutions.

Adopting ethical practices is essential for businesses. Forming ethics committees to oversee AI and automated system development ensures adherence to ethical standards. Engaging with stakeholders, including customers, employees, and regulators, helps maintain transparency and accountability.

Role of Governments - Developing and enforcing comprehensive cyber laws is a critical responsibility of governments. Implementing data protection legislation ensures the privacy and security of personal data.

Supporting education and workforce development through initiatives that promote digital literacy and skills development is vital. Creating job training programs prepares workers for careers in the digital economy.

Promoting innovation and research is essential for government roles. Providing funding and grants to support research and development in digital technologies encourages progress. Fostering public-private partnerships drives innovation and addresses digital challenges.

Preparing for future digital challenges requires a multi-faceted approach involving individuals, businesses, and governments. By focusing on cybersecurity, digital literacy, data protection, ethical AI, regulatory frameworks, resilience against disinformation, and fostering innovation, society can effectively navigate and thrive in the evolving digital landscape. Continuous learning, adaptability, and proactive measures are key to staying ahead of digital challenges and leveraging the benefits of emerging technologies.

243

CHAPTER LX

Innovations in AI for Enhancing Digital Safety

Artificial Intelligence (AI) is revolutionizing digital safety by providing advanced tools and techniques to detect, prevent, and respond to cyber threats. Innovations in AI are enhancing security measures, protecting personal data, and ensuring a safer online environment. This guide explores some of the latest AI innovations that are making significant strides in digital safety.

Key AI Innovations in Digital Safety - AI-powered threat detection and response systems are at the forefront of enhancing digital safety. Behavioral analytics allow AI systems to analyze user behavior, detecting anomalies that may indicate a security breach. By understanding typical user behavior, AI can identify deviations that suggest malicious activity. Additionally, automated incident response mechanisms enable AI to isolate compromised systems, block malicious IP addresses, and alert security teams swiftly, reducing the impact of cyber threats.

Machine learning for malware detection employs advanced pattern recognition to identify malware, even those not previously encountered. This capability allows for the detection of zero-day exploits and sophisticated attacks. These systems continuously learn from new data, improving their ability to detect emerging threats over time, thus providing a robust defense against malware.

Natural Language Processing (NLP) is pivotal in phishing detection. NLP algorithms analyze the content of emails and messages to detect phishing attempts. By understanding the context and identifying suspicious patterns, AI can flag potential phishing attacks and provide real-time alerts to users, helping prevent credential theft and other malicious activities.

Biometric authentication, driven by AI, offers enhanced security measures such as facial recognition, fingerprint scanning, and voice recognition. These methods provide an additional layer of security for user accounts and sensitive systems. Continuous authentication, where AI continuously verifies user identity throughout a session, further enhances security for sensitive operations.

AI is also revolutionizing network security. Intrusion Detection Systems (IDS) powered by AI monitor network traffic for signs of suspicious activity, such as unusual data transfers or access attempts, and respond accordingly. Machine learning models detect anomalies in network behavior that may indicate a breach or attack, enabling proactive threat mitigation.

Data privacy and protection are significantly enhanced by AI. Automated data anonymization ensures privacy while allowing data to be used for analysis and research. Privacy-preserving computation techniques, such as homomorphic encryption, enable computations on encrypted data without exposing the data itself, thus enhancing data security.

AI-driven content moderation employs automated filtering systems that can remove harmful content, such as hate speech, violence, and explicit material, from online platforms. NLP and image recognition technologies help AI understand the context of content, ensuring more accurate moderation and creating safer online environments.

In fraud detection, AI systems monitor financial transactions in real-time, detecting and flagging suspicious activities indicative of fraud. Machine learning models assign risk scores to transactions and user behaviors, helping organizations prioritize their response efforts and mitigate fraud effectively.

AI in cyber threat intelligence employs predictive analysis to foresee potential cyber threats by analyzing vast amounts of data from various sources, including dark web forums, social media, and threat databases. AI-driven tools assist security analysts in proactively hunting for threats within an organization's network, identifying vulnerabilities before they can be exploited.

Applications and Benefits - These AI innovations bring numerous benefits. Enhanced security for businesses through proactive threat mitigation and reduced response time is significant. Businesses can leverage AI to identify and mitigate threats before they cause significant damage, and automated incident response minimizes the time between threat detection and action, reducing the impact of cyber attacks.

Improved user safety online is another benefit, with real-time detection and alerting systems helping users avoid phishing attacks and protect their personal information. Automated filtering ensures safer online environments by reducing exposure to harmful content.

AI also strengthens data protection by helping organizations comply with data privacy regulations through AI-driven data anonymization and privacy-preserving techniques. Ensuring data privacy while enabling secure data usage for analysis and decision-making is crucial.

For security teams, AI increases efficiency by augmenting their capabilities, allowing them to focus on complex and high-priority tasks. Automation reduces the need for manual intervention, optimizing resource allocation and reducing operational costs.

Challenges and Considerations - Despite these benefits, AI in digital safety presents challenges. Algorithmic bias can lead to unfair outcomes, making it essential to ensure fairness and transparency in AI algorithms. Regular audits, diverse training datasets, and fairness metrics can help mitigate bias.

Privacy concerns arise with extensive data collection for AI systems, necessitating transparent and ethical data practices. Obtaining informed consent from users for data collection and usage is crucial for maintaining trust.

Implementing AI solutions can be technically challenging, requiring expertise and resources. Ensuring seamless integration with existing security infrastructure is critical for effective deployment.

Future Directions - Advancements in AI research will lead to more advanced and effective security solutions. Continuous improvement through ongoing research and development will drive these advancements. Interdisciplinary collaboration between AI researchers, cybersecurity experts, and policymakers will be essential for innovation and addressing emerging challenges.

Developing standardized guidelines and frameworks for AI in cybersecurity will ensure consistent and effective practices. Establishing ethical guidelines for AI development and deployment will ensure responsible use and protect user rights.

Investing in education and training programs to develop skills in AI and cybersecurity is crucial for building a capable workforce. Raising public awareness about digital safety and AI technologies will empower users to protect themselves online.

Innovations in AI are playing a pivotal role in enhancing digital safety, offering advanced tools for threat detection, data protection, and user security. By leveraging AI technologies, individuals, businesses, and governments can proactively address cyber threats and create a safer digital environment. However, addressing challenges related to bias, privacy, and implementation is crucial for realizing the full potential of AI in digital safety. Continuous advancements, interdisciplinary collaboration, and robust regulatory frameworks will shape the future of AI-driven digital security.

Conclusion

CHAPTER LXI

Summarizing Key Points

The rapid advancement of digital technologies, particularly Artificial Intelligence (AI), presents both opportunities and challenges. As society becomes increasingly reliant on digital platforms, ensuring digital safety is paramount. This summary outlines key strategies, innovations, and considerations for enhancing digital safety in this evolving landscape.

Innovations in AI for Digital Safety - AI-powered threat detection and response systems are critical in enhancing digital safety. Behavioral analytics detect anomalies in user behavior to identify potential security breaches, while automated incident response mechanisms swiftly address threats, reducing response time and mitigating damage. Machine learning for malware detection employs advanced pattern recognition to identify new and emerging malware by recognizing specific patterns and signatures, continuously improving detection capabilities with more data.

Natural Language Processing (NLP) plays a vital role in phishing detection by analyzing the content of emails and messages for phishing indicators and providing real-time alerts to users about potential phishing attempts. Biometric authentication enhances security through the use of facial recognition, fingerprint scanning, and voice recognition for secure authentication, with continuous authentication verifying identity throughout user sessions.

In network security, AI-driven intrusion detection systems (IDS) monitor network traffic for suspicious activities, while anomaly detection identifies unusual network behavior that may indicate a security threat. Data privacy and protection are significantly enhanced by AI through data anonymization, ensuring privacy while allowing data analysis, and privacy-preserving computation, which enables secure computations on encrypted data.

AI also revolutionizes content moderation by automating the filtering of harmful content such as hate speech and explicit material, using NLP and image recognition for accurate content moderation. In fraud detection, AI systems monitor financial transactions in real-time to detect suspicious activities and assign risk levels to transactions and user behaviors. AI in cyber threat intelligence employs predictive analysis to anticipate potential threats by analyzing vast data sources and assists in proactively identifying vulnerabilities.

Applications and Benefits - The applications of these AI innovations bring numerous benefits, including enhanced security for businesses through proactive threat mitigation and reduced response time, improving overall security measures. User safety online is improved with phishing prevention systems that alert users to phishing attempts and content moderation that creates safer online environments by filtering harmful content. Data protection is strengthened as AI helps organizations comply with privacy regulations and ensures secure data usage for analysis.

For security teams, AI increases efficiency by augmenting their capabilities, allowing them to focus on complex and high-priority tasks, and optimizing resources by reducing the need for manual intervention.

Challenges and Considerations - Despite these benefits, several challenges and considerations need to be addressed. AI systems can inherit biases from training data, leading to unfair outcomes, necessitating regular audits and the use of diverse datasets to mitigate biases. Privacy concerns arise with extensive data collection required for AI systems, emphasizing the need for transparent and ethical data practices and ensuring informed user consent for data collection and usage.

Implementing AI solutions poses technical challenges, requiring expertise and resources, and ensuring seamless integration with existing systems is crucial for effective deployment.

Future Directions - Future directions involve continuous advancements in AI research, which will lead to more effective security solutions and interdisciplinary collaboration that drives innovation. Developing standardized global guidelines and regulatory frameworks for AI in cybersecurity ensures consistent practices and establishing ethical guidelines for AI development and deployment guarantees responsible use and protection of user rights.

Investing in education and training programs to develop skills in AI and cybersecurity is essential for building a capable workforce. Public awareness campaigns about digital safety and AI technologies will empower users to protect themselves online.

Innovations in AI are significantly enhancing digital safety by providing advanced tools for threat detection, data protection, and user security. Addressing challenges related to bias, privacy, and implementation is crucial for leveraging AI to create a safer digital environment. Continuous advancements, collaboration, and robust regulatory frameworks will be essential in shaping the future of AI-driven digital safety.

CHAPTER LXII

Empowering Teens for a Safe Digital Journey

As digital natives, teens are growing up in an increasingly connected world. While the internet offers numerous opportunities for learning, socializing, and entertainment, it also presents risks such as cyberbullying, privacy breaches, and exposure to inappropriate content. Empowering teens with the knowledge and tools to navigate the digital world safely is crucial for their well-being. This guide provides strategies to help teens manage their online presence responsibly.

Key Strategies for Empowering Teens - Education and awareness are the foundation of empowering teens for a safe digital journey. Educate teens about the potential risks of the internet, including cyberbullying, identity theft, and exposure to inappropriate content. Teach them how to critically evaluate information online, recognize fake news, and understand the implications of their digital footprint.

Encouraging safe online practices is essential. Teach teens to use privacy settings on social media and other online platforms to control who can see their information. Emphasize the importance of creating strong, unique passwords and changing them regularly. Make sure they understand the risks of sharing personal information, such as addresses, phone numbers, and financial details online.

Dealing with cyberbullying requires recognition and support. Help teens identify the signs of cyberbullying, which can include harassment, exclusion, and spreading rumors. Encourage them to report cyberbullying to trusted adults, school authorities, or the relevant platform and provide emotional support throughout the process.

Managing digital footprints is another critical area. Teach teens to consider the long-term implications of their online posts, as digital footprints can impact their future education and career opportunities. Encourage regular reviews and cleanups of old posts and photos that may no longer represent their current values or identity.

Promote a healthy online-offline balance by helping teens set reasonable limits on their screen time to ensure they have a balanced lifestyle that includes offline activities. Encourage participation in physical activities, hobbies, and face-to-face interactions to reduce dependency on digital devices.

Safe social media use is vital for teens. Discuss the potential risks associated with social media, including exposure to inappropriate content and the impact on self-esteem. Encourage positive interactions online, emphasizing the importance of supporting others and promoting kindness.

Navigating online friendships requires caution. Teach teens to verify the identities of people they interact with online and to be cautious about accepting friend requests or engaging with strangers. If meeting online friends in person, ensure it is in a public place and with parental consent.

Protecting against online scams is crucial. Educate teens on how to recognize phishing emails and messages that seek to steal personal information. Teach them to avoid clicking on suspicious links and downloading attachments from unknown sources.

Tools and Resources for Teens - Parental control apps are valuable tools for monitoring online activity, setting screen time limits, and blocking inappropriate content. Apps like Qustodio, Norton Family, and Net Nanny offer comprehensive parental control features. Educational websites and programs, such as digital citizenship courses, teach responsible online behavior and critical thinking. Direct teens to resources like Common Sense Media and Cyberbullying Research Center for guidance on digital safety.

Support networks play a significant role. Encourage teens to participate in peer support groups where they can share experiences and strategies for staying safe online. Support school initiatives that focus on digital literacy and online safety education.

Encouraging Open Communication - Creating a safe environment is key to open communication. Foster an environment where teens feel comfortable discussing their online experiences without fear of judgment or punishment. Make it a habit to regularly check in with teens about their online activities and any concerns they may have.

Active listening involves showing genuine interest in their online world, including the games they play, the social media platforms they use, and the content they consume. Provide support and guidance rather than simply setting rules, helping them understand the reasons behind safe online practices.

Collaborative rule-setting is effective in gaining compliance. Involve teens in setting rules for internet use. This collaborative approach makes them more likely to adhere to the rules. Clearly explain the reasons behind each rule and the potential consequences of not following them.

Empowering teens for a safe digital journey involves education, awareness, and open communication. By teaching safe online practices, promoting a healthy online-offline balance, and providing the necessary tools and resources, we can help teens navigate the digital world responsibly and confidently. Engaging in continuous dialogue and offering support are key to ensuring teens' digital safety and well-being.